"This is an essential companion for researchers on domestic and sexual violence. Whether their data comprises voices, numbers, images, or something else, new and established researchers alike will find invaluable guidance on effective ways to generate new knowledge and use this to make a difference."

Dr Michael Flood, author of *Engaging Men and Boys in Violence Prevention*

"This timely and authoritative book is an immensely readable account of the philosophies, principles and practices of feminist-informed methodologies used in researching gender-based violence. It engages with critical questions of theory, politics and ethics and through its use of case studies and the provision of excellent examples of the application of feminist research will no doubt excite and inspire both new and experienced researchers."

Michele Burman, Professor of Criminology, University of Glasgow

RESEARCHING GENDER, VIOLENCE AND ABUSE

Feminist research on gender, violence and abuse has been an area of academic study since the late 1970s, and has increased exponentially over this time on a global scale. Although situated in a predominantly qualitative tradition, research in the field has developed to include quantitative and mixed methodologies. This book offers a compendium of research methods on gender and violence, from the traditional to the innovative, and showcases best practice in feminist research and international case studies. *Researching Gender, Violence and Abuse* covers:

- The origins of feminist research,
- Ethical considerations relating to research on gender, violence and abuse,
- Working in partnership with organisations such as the police or the voluntary sector,
- A comprehensive range of research methods including interviews and focus groups, surveys, arts-based research and ethnography,
- The challenges and opportunities of working with existing data,
- The influence of activism on research and the translation of research into policy and practice.

This book is perfect reading for students taking courses on violence against women, domestic violence, gender and crime, as well as advanced students embarking on new research.

Nicole Westmarland is Director of Durham University Centre for Research into Violence and Abuse (CRiVA), where she is also Professor of Criminology and Head of Department of Sociology. She has researched a range of different forms of violence against women and is deeply committed to conducting research that can create real world change. She is Vice Chair of Darlington and Co. Durham Rape and Sexual Abuse Counselling Centre. She is the author of a number of books and articles, including *Violence Against Women: Criminological Perspectives on Men's Violences* (Routledge).

Hannah Bows is Deputy Director of CRiVA and Assistant Professor in Criminal Law at Durham Law School. Her research focuses on different forms of violence against women, particularly domestic and sexual violence. Her recent work includes a national study of rape against older people, a national study profiling homicide of older people and a study exploring 'risk' in relation to older sex offenders and policing. Outside of the university, she is the deputy director of the BSC Victims Network, Chair of Age UK Teesside and sits as a Magistrate on the Durham and Darlington bench.

RESEARCHING GENDER, VIOLENCE AND ABUSE

Theory, Methods, Action

Nicole Westmarland
and Hannah Bows

 Routledge
Taylor & Francis Group

LONDON AND NEW YORK

First published 2019
by Routledge
2 Park Square, Milton Park, Abingdon, Oxon OX14 4RN

and by Routledge
52 Vanderbilt Avenue, New York, NY 10017

Routledge is an imprint of the Taylor & Francis Group, an informa business

British Library Cataloguing-in-Publication Data
A catalogue record for this book is available from the British Library

Library of Congress Cataloging-in-Publication Data
Names: Westmarland, Nicole, author. | Bows, Hannah, author.
Title: Researching gender, violence and abuse: theory, methods, action / Nicole Westmarland and Hannah Bows.
Description: Abingdon, Oxon; New York, NY: Routledge, 2019. | Includes bibliographical references and index.
Identifiers: LCCN 2018030861 | ISBN 9781138641259 (hardback) | ISBN 9781138641266 (pbk.) | ISBN 9781315630618 (ebook)
Subjects: LCSH: Women's studies−Methodology. | Feminism−Research−Methodology. | Sex role−Research−Methodology. | Women−Violence against−Research−Methodology.
Classification: LCC HQ1180 .W475 2019 | DDC 305.4201−dc23
LC record available at https://lccn.loc.gov/2018030861

ISBN: 978-1-138-64125-9 (hbk)
ISBN: 978-1-138-64126-6 (pbk)
ISBN: 978-1-315-63061-8 (ebk)

Typeset in Interstate
by Apex CoVantage, LLC
Printed and bound by CPI Group (UK) Ltd, Croydon, CRO 4YY

CONTENTS

ACKNOWLEDGEMENTS

We would like to thank our colleagues at Durham University Centre for Research into Violence and Abuse (CRiVA). Being around such excellent, enthusiastic, mainly early career scholars is an exciting place to be. We are grateful for the continued support and contribution to our feminist, collegiate environment that each member brings to the Centre in different ways. We are particularly grateful to Lizzy Kirkham and to Stephen Burrell for their support in the later stages of the preparation of this book – stepping up to help us at our time of need – feminist solidarity in action! We are also grateful to fellow feminist academic tweeters across the world who helped us locate some of the case studies that went on to be included in this book. Our thanks also go to Hannah Catterall from Routledge for her patience with us.

On a personal note, Hannah would like to thank her golden retriever (Rufus). His daily walks provide much needed thinking space and many of these chapters were mentally put together whilst out walking with him.

Nicole feels she should probably thank her children (Oscar Westmarland-Morrison (age 8) and Otis Westmarland (age 2)) for making sure she never meets her deadlines (don't write the book, play instead Mummy!), doesn't waste her life sleeping (never slept through yet!) and generally being too adorable to stay cross with for long.

1 Introduction

Few social scientists would cite research methods as the most interesting part of their role. However, as discussed in this book, research methods represent an area which is ripe for innovation and development. Furthermore, a thorough understanding of research methods can provide a solid grounding for research which supports impactful work in a climate of scarce resources. And it is not just academic life that the importance of understanding research methods and methodology can prove useful. Being able to critically read and evaluate research through a thorough understanding of the whole of the research process has allowed the authors as academics and citizens to navigate their lives outside of work in a more evidence-based manner. For example, whilst on maternity leave, one of the authors (Westmarland) drew on her research skills to assess the risks and benefits of taking different medications during pregnancy and whilst breastfeeding and was able to make an evidence-based decision on bed sharing with a baby. Hence, the importance of being able to understand and evaluate the usefulness of different options in different contexts represents an essential part of many people's daily lives.

This book is not a 'how to' guide to doing feminist research on gender, violence and abuse, nor is it intended to be prescriptive about what the 'right' methods may be. Instead, it aims to provide inspiration, both for new researchers who are just starting out and for experienced researchers who are looking to diversify their methodological approach. Some of the feminist researchers that the authors consider to be the most exciting in terms of methodological innovation are those at the entry stage of their careers. In light of this, this book draws frequently on examples of good practice from early career and PhD research.

Method(s) for researching gender, violence and abuse

Methods can be described as research tools which stem from methodologies (Giddings, 2006). In social science, research has typically been conducted using either quantitative or qualitative methods, with the two methods having been viewed as mutually antagonistic ideal types which represent different paradigms of social science itself (Bryman, 1988). Of these two methods, qualitative methods have traditionally been the preferred research methods of feminist researchers in their attempts to achieve the commitments outlined in the previous section. By contrast, quantitative methods were perceived by feminist researchers in the 1970s and 1980s as being aligned with 'malestream' social research and were largely rejected by the feminist movement. This led to something of a paradigm war (Oakley, 1999).

'Malestream' social research was criticised during the 1970s and 1980s for not fully incorporating women and consequently producing knowledge which did not relate to women or their concerns (Tolman and Szalacha, 1999). Feminist criticisms of quantitative methods were made on several grounds: that the choice of topics often implicitly supported sexist values; that female subjects were excluded or marginalised; that relations between researcher and researched were intrinsically exploitative; that the resulting data were superficial and overgeneralised; and that quantitative research was generally not used to overcome social problems (Oakley, 1999). Furthermore, it was argued that quantitative research presented a distorted view of the world a view which was dominated by male ideology and limited by issues such as reliability and representativeness (Sarantakos, 2013). Thus, feminist research at that time was generally considered to be different from and incompatible with conventional quantitative social research and science (Sarantakos, 2013).

In light of this, initial feminist contributions to discussion of research methods were focused on qualitative research techniques (e.g. Oakley, 1981; Finch, 1993). However, more recently feminists have argued that quantitative research methods have a role to play within feminist methodology (Kelly et al., 1994; Sampson et al., 2008). The sole reliance on qualitative methods has been challenged by a number of feminist researchers since the 1990s (see, for example, Gelsthorpe, 1992; Maynard and Purvis, 1994; Westmarland, 2001), and the positive uses of quantitative research methods in feminist research has now been evidenced and documented (Jayaratne, 1983; Walby and Myhill, 2001). It is sometimes wrongly assumed that feminist researchers take an anti-quantitative position and therefore abstain from quantitative standards and principles of research such as validity, objectivity, reliability and generalisation (Sarantakos, 2013). Sarantakos (2013) states that, whilst some feminists may take this position, in the majority of cases, the assumption that feminist researchers do not see any value in quantitative research is not correct.

The need to move beyond the paradigm war between quantitative and qualitative approaches was argued by Oakley (1999). Oakley (1999) suggests that the priority for feminist researchers should be to take a more critical and ethical approach to all kinds of methods, whether quantitative or qualitative. Ultimately, it is increasingly acknowledged that the difference between feminist and non-feminist research lies not in the type of methods they use, but in the way they choose and utilise conventional methods to meet their research goals (Kelly et al., 2005; Sarantakos, 2013). A significant number of feminist researchers now utilise a mixed-method approach which, it is argued, is able to provide both the big picture and the personal story (Hodgkin, 2008). Moreover, it has been argued in the existing feminist literature that feminist research which draws evidence from a variety of sources and methods is more likely to be seen as valid and reliable, and thus more likely to be heard in the policy arena (Shapiro et al., 2003). Combining quantitative methods such as questionnaires with qualitative methods such as interviews allows feminist criminological researchers to examine the extent of violence as well as the lived experiences of those who have been victims of violence. Furthermore, a mixed-method approach increases the likelihood that researchers will gain a broad and in-depth understanding of the topic they are investigating, which in turn will help them to persuade others of the veracity of their findings (Reinharz and Davidman, 1992).

Summary of the book

The remainder of the book is divided into three parts. Part I builds on this introductory chapter to consider feminist methodologies and approaches in practice. Chapter 2 provides an overview of the feminist principles which underpin gender, violence and abuse research. In Chapter 3, key ethical considerations in conducting gender, violence and abuse research are discussed, providing an overview of some of the key debates in relation to conducting 'sensitive' research with 'vulnerable' participants. Chapter 4 examines how feminist research on gender, violence and abuse has begun to work in more pragmatic ways with different disciplines and organisations. This chapter considers the opportunities and challenges of working within and across different disciplines.

Part II of the book is dedicated to showcasing innovative methods in feminist research. Each chapter in this part of the book utilises case studies to demonstrate the ways these innovative methods have been applied in recent research. Chapter 5 focuses on two commonly used qualitative methods, interviews and focus groups. These methods were traditionally the first choice in feminist research and continue to be two of the most widely used methods. This chapter features the work of one of the authors (Bows) who used interviews to explore older women's experiences of rape. The chapter focuses on issues related to engaging in research as an 'outsider,' as well as the impact of age differences between a researcher and their participants. A second case study showcases the work of Burrell (Durham) who used focus groups with members of men's sports teams at one university to explore how men understand intimate partner violence prevention campaigns.

Although traditionally criticised for being 'malestream,' surveys are an important method in violence and abuse research. Chapter 6 examines some of the most frequently used surveys, including the Crime Survey for England and Wales (CSEW), which has included a specific module on domestic violence, sexual violence and stalking since 2004/05. Case studies include the use of campus climate surveys to gather data on the prevalence of sexual violence at US universities.

Art-based and creative methods have a long history in feminist research, although they have increased in popularity over the last decade or so as technology has also developed exponentially. Photovoice, poetry and pottery are just three examples of the methods that fall within the categories of arts-based and creative methods described in Chapter 7. Case studies include a recent project by McGarry (Nottingham) who utilised pottery as a method to explore women's experiences of female genital mutilation.

Whilst researchers are often looking for innovative ways to generate new data, they are increasingly being encouraged to make use of existing data sets. Chapter 8 explores the ways in which academics are utilising existing data to address new research aims and questions. Whilst this chapter primarily considers the ways in which researchers access and analyse data that has been made available through published reports, data sets or repositories, examples of quasi-secondary data analysis are also considered. For example, the use of Freedom of Information requests to access data held (but not published) by public bodies in the UK has been a key research method for the authors of this book over the last few years.

In Chapter 9, ethnography and observation are examined. Although used by feminist researchers across a range of social sciences, these methods are perhaps most commonly used in anthropology, sociology and public health research. Examples in this chapter include doctoral research by Johnson (Durham) who conducted observations of domestic violence refuges in Scotland.

Part III looks at how feminist research and theory is used in policy and practice. Chapter 10 demonstrates the ways in which gender, violence and abuse researchers have worked alongside, and as, activists. Chapter 11 explores the way research findings have been translated into policy and practice. Case studies include work by McGlynn (Durham) who worked with colleagues to develop understandings of revenge porn and extreme pornography. This resulted in a new conceptualisation of these forms of violence against women as 'image based sexual abuse.' This concept has been influential and informed legislative and policy developments in this field. On a practical level, Lombard's work in Scotland exploring attitudes of primary school children to men's violence against women led to the commissioning of training for secondary school head teachers and teaching staff which was rolled out across more than 20 secondary schools in Scotland.

Finally, in the Afterword, we briefly reflect on the diverse range of methods and innovative approaches that feminist researchers are using to examine gender, violence and abuse. This chapter draws together the key themes that emerge from this book and considers future directions for feminist methods and research.

References

Bryman, A. (1988) *Quantity and Quality in Social Research*. London: Unwin Hyman.

Dickson-Swift, V., James, E. L., Kippen, S. and Liamputtong, P. (2007) Doing sensitive research: What challenges do qualitative researchers face?, *Qualitative Research*, 7(3), pp. 327–353.

Finch, J. (1993) 'It's great to have someone to talk to': The ethics and politics of interviewing women, In: M. Hammersley (Ed.) *Social Research Philosophy Politics and Practice* (pp. 166–180). London: Sage.

Gelsthorpe, L. (1992) Response to Martyn Hammersley's paper 'On feminist methodology', *Sociology*, 26(2), pp. 213–218.

Giddings, L. S. (2006) Mixed-methods research: Positivism dressed in drag?, *Journal of Research in Nursing*, 11(3), pp. 195–203.

Hodgkin, S. (2008) Telling it all: A story of women's social capital using a mixed methods approach, *Journal of Mixed Methods Research*, 2(4), pp. 296–316.

Jayaratne, T. E. (1983) The value of quantitative methodology for feminist research, In: G. Bowles and R. D. Klein (Eds.) *Theories of Women's Studies* (pp. 140–162). London: Routledge & Kegan Paul.

Kelly, L., Burton, S. and Regan, L. (1994) Researching women's lives or studying women's oppression? Reflections on what constitutes feminist research, In: M. Maynard and J. Purvis. (Eds.) *Researching Women's Lives from a Feminist Perspective* (pp. 27–48). London: Taylor & Francis.

Kelly, L., Lovett, J. and Regan, L. (2005) *A Gap or a Chasm? Attrition in Reported Rape Cases*. London: Home Office.

Maynard, M. and Purvis, J. (Eds.) (1994) *Researching Women's Lives from a Feminist Perspective* (pp. 27–48). London: Taylor and Francis.

Oakley, A. (1981) Interviewing women: a contradiction in terms, In: Helen Roberts (Ed.) *Doing Feminist Research* (pp. 30–62). London: Routledge and Kegan Paul.

Oakley, A. (1999) Paradigm wars: Some thoughts on a personal and public trajectory, *International Journal of Social Research Methodology*, 2(3), pp. 247–254.

Reinharz, S. and Davidman, L. (1992) *Feminist Methods in Social Research*. Oxford: Oxford University Press.

Sampson, H., Bloor, M. and Fincham, B. (2008) A price worth paying?: Considering the 'cost' of reflexive research methods and the influence of feminist ways of 'doing', *Sociology*, 42(5), pp. 919–933.

Sarantakos, S. (2013) *Social Research*. Basingstoke: Palgrave Macmillan.

Shapiro, M., Setterlund, D. and Cragg, C. (2003) Capturing the complexity of women's experiences: A mixed-method approach to studying incontinence in older women, *Affilia*, *18*(1), pp. 21-33.

Tolman, D. L. and Szalacha, L. A. (1999) Dimensions of desire: Bridging qualitative and quantitative methods in a study of female adolescent sexuality, *Psychology of Women Quarterly*, *23*(1), pp. 7-39.

Walby, S. and Myhill, A. (2001) New survey methodologies in researching violence against women, *British Journal of Criminology*, *41*(3), pp. 502-522.

Westmarland, N. (2001) The quantitative/qualitative debate and feminist research: A subjective view of objectivity, *Forum: Qualitative Social Research*, *2*(1), Art. 13.

PART I

Feminist approaches to research

2 The principles of feminist research

A high proportion of research on gender, violence and abuse comes from a feminist perspective. Hence, it is important in a book of this nature to consider what is meant by the term 'feminist.' Just as there is no single definition of feminism, there is also no one definition of feminist research. However, it is important to be able to identify the key elements of feminist research in order to understand the underlying theories and to advance feminist causes. There has been much debate over what makes research 'feminist.' Moreover, there have been similar debates surrounding the methods employed by feminist research, including whether a given methodology or method can be classed as inherently 'feminist.' This chapter will begin by providing a brief historical overview of the emergence of feminist research and of the key conceptual and methodological debates which have shaped this work over the last few decades. These debates will then be brought up to date with a discussion of the core principles which underpin the myriad of approaches, and which unify the various streams of feminist research.

Defining feminism and feminist theory

A definition of feminist research requires an understanding of the feminist theory which underlies it. Feminist theory is wide and diverse, with no singular definition; indeed, there are numerous divisions both within and between 'feminisms' (Westmarland, 2001). However, despite these differences, there are nevertheless a number of core themes which underlie the various branches of feminist theory. Feminism is concerned with the basic structures and ideologies that oppress women; it seeks to highlight the ubiquity of gender stereotypes and women's global inequality (Brooks and Hesse-Biber, 2007). Feminist theory challenges the assumption that knowledge which is built upon the experiences of men (the dominant group) can be used to understand the experiences of women and other oppressed groups of people (Hesse-Biber, 2012). Stanley and Wise (2002) suggest that feminist theories typically embody three key themes: the central and common belief that women are oppressed; the acceptance that the 'personal is political' (women's experiences of oppression are located in broader socio-political frameworks); and a sense of 'feminist consciousness,' broadly defined as being aware of and challenging gender inequality (Aronson, 2017). However, they note that whilst these themes are apparent throughout feminist theory, there remains ongoing debate about what these themes actually mean, and what consequences they have for feminist research.

The history of feminist research

In order to examine the ways in which feminist theory translates into feminist research, it is useful to examine the development of feminist research and methodology over time. Feminist research has its origins within various disciplines, two of which are criminology and sociology. Until the 1970s, criminology was primarily comprised of research conducted by men, about men, for men. This approach became known as 'malestream' criminology (see Smart, 1995; Morris and Gelsthorpe, 1991). In the late 1960s, scholars began to draw attention to the omission of women from general theories of crime. Second wave feminists argued that theories to explain female victimology and criminality were inadequate; whilst women were not entirely absent from this work, their rare incorporation into theory was narrowly restricted to biological arguments and centred around what are now termed 'double deviancy' theories (where women are not only punished for their offending but also for being a woman, Daly and Chesney-Lind, 1988). Similar to criminology, sociology was also criticised for its failure to discuss the experiences of women. Feminists argued that the discipline was sexist as it had grown out of the male society, thus focusing only on the activities and interests of men (e.g. Oakley, 1974).

As these critiques of male bias in criminology and sociology began to take shape, feminists sought to make changes both within these fields and in the broader academic context, challenging gender-based law, policy and practice. Initially, this work was fronted by women under the branch of 'radical' feminism. However, the differences in beliefs and approaches led to the development of a number of branches of feminist inquiry, including liberal feminism, Marxist feminism, standpoint feminist, and later, intersectional feminism. Feminist research, therefore, includes various branches of feminist thought, each of which represent different perspectives and assumptions about the causes of gender inequality. These branches are united, however, in their focus on women's oppression and their drive for social change (Daly and Chesney-Lind, 1988).

Core characteristics and aims of feminist research

Rhode (1990) states that, although feminist research differs widely in many respects, the theories that underpin this research share three central commitments; political, substantive and methodological. On a political level, they seek to promote equality between women and men. On a substantive level, they make gender a focus of analysis. Finally, on a methodological level, they aspire to describe the world in ways that correspond to women's experience, and seek to identify the fundamental social transformations necessary for full equality between the sexes.

At the centre of feminist research lies a commitment to giving a voice to the marginalised. Hesse-Biber (2012) suggests the central mission of feminist researchers should be to conduct research on behalf of women and other oppressed groups. As such, the lived experiences of women are prioritised through research which focuses on women as the sources of knowledge (Campbell and Wasco, 2000) and provides practical benefits for the group being researched. As Letherby (2003) states, feminism is both theory and practice. Feminist researchers have a political commitment to produce useful knowledge that will make a difference to women's lives. Whilst other research is about women, feminist research is beneficial for women as well as being about them (Dickson-Swift et al., 2007).

The principles of feminist research

Methodology refers to how social investigations should be approached (Ramazanoglu and Holland, 2002). As there is no unified feminist theory, there is also no single feminist methodology. When adopting a feminist methodological framework 'it is crucial to bear in mind that feminist research is a "perspective"' (Reinharz and Davidman, 1992, p. 84) rather than a clearly defined methodology. As Ramazanoglu and Holland (2002, p. 10) state, 'Feminists are divided over where ideas come from, how people make sense of their experience and what evidence is evidence of.' Rather than offering a distinct methodology, feminist research and scholarship provides the researcher with a broad methodological and ethical framework for conducting research with women, for women.

Beckman (2014) suggests that there are eight core feminist principles which unite the various feminist theories and methodologies, in turn influencing the methods that are used to research gender, violence and abuse. These principles are: addressing power imbalances; expanding the questions asked; listening to women's voices and experiences; incorporating diversity and intersectionality; conducting multidisciplinary and mixed methods research; being reflexive; building social relationships in the research process; and using research results. The following section discusses each of these principles in turn.

Addressing power imbalances

One of the fundamental commitments in feminist research generally, but particularly important in research on violence and abuse, has been to address and reduce hierarchies and power imbalances in the research process. Feminist research is committed to removing these hierarchal relationships through methods which allow for reflexive, reciprocal dialogue that prioritises the words and lived experiences of participants and minimises the potential for participants to be simply 'used' as a tool in the data collection process. Traditional quantitative social research methods were heavily criticised by feminists in the 1970s and 1980s for constructing and maintaining research hierarchies. These hierarchies arose as a consequence of the dichotomous relationship between researcher and participant; researchers typically had control over the research, methods and data collection, whilst the participant lacked control, acting instead as a passive giver of information. As Campbell and Wasco state,

> Traditionally, a hierarchy existed between researcher and researched: the researcher is the 'all-knowing' expert, the participant is not; the researcher has access to all information about the study, the participant does not.
>
> (Campbell and Wasco, 2000, p. 786)

Fontes (2004) argues that researchers usually study down the power hierarchy; typically researchers study those who are poorer, are less educated, are more discriminated against, have poorer health and possess less social power than themselves. Arguably, power disparities exist in many research scenarios, with participants having little control over the questions, research directions, modes of inquiry or the knowledge that is produced. However, it should be noted that hierarchy within research is not as linear as often described. Whereas it has traditionally been assumed that the researcher holds the dominant position of power within the interview hierarchal relationship, research has recently noted the fluidity of power dynamics within the interview (Tang, 2002). The balance of power is not fixed and may vary according to how particular respondents are recruited into the study and the age and status of the women being interviewed (Cotterill, 1992 cited in Tang, 2002). One ethical issue is that of power and the complex dynamics which emerge during a qualitative interview (Robertson and Hale, 2011).

Feminists have sought to reduce the power imbalances which can occur within research. Building trust, conducting research with women, for women, rather than doing research 'to women' has therefore been a central commitment of feminist research. This commitment is reflected in the methods they use to research gender, violence and abuse. Traditionally, interviews were preferred by feminist researchers (e.g. Oakley, 1988) as a way of facilitating reciprocal conversations with women about their experiences of violence. As outlined in Chapter 4, different types of research interviews exist, including structured, unstructured, life course and biographical interviews. Interviews, as well as focus groups, can be used to explore subjective meaning and lived experience of women (and men) by situating the participants as the experts and holders of knowledge, and by encouraging reciprocal conversation between the researcher and participant.

Although interviews and focus groups have often been favoured by feminist researchers as a method that allows for the reduction of hierarchical power relations, there are also other methods that can be used to minimise such imbalances. Chapters 6 and 8 document the way arts-based methods and ethnography are used to research gender, violence and abuse. Both of these methods have been used in violence and abuse research with 'hard to reach' and/or marginalised groups, whose voices are less often heard. Being willing to adapt research methods to the population that is being researched – so that it is the researcher that is being flexible and adaptable rather than the participant – is particularly important. This willingness can be rewarding in terms of being able to engage with victim-survivors of violence and abuse who may not be willing or able to participate in other forms of research such as surveys.

Expanding the questions asked

According to Beckman (2014), expanding the questions asked by research, and, crucially, reframing the way existing questions are asked, is a fundamental principle in feminist research. This requires researchers to consider broader social structural issues when designing their research questions. For example, rather than asking why women stay in abusive relationships, researchers should consider the broad socio-cultural macro and micro issues that prevent women from leaving abusive relationships. Another example of reframing within feminist research is Stark's (2007) emphasis on the need to recognise women's right to freedom as well as to safety when considering the topic of men's coercive control.

In the late 2000s/early 2010s, we (Westmarland) worked with Liz Kelly to try to redraw the boundaries which were used to determine whether domestic violence perpetrator programmes were seen as being 'successful' or 'unsuccessful.' The researchers were keen to 'expand the questions' asked by providing a critique of the narrowness of previous studies of domestic violence perpetrator programmes, and recasting the core of the research question at stake. They were initially commissioned to investigate the research question 'do perpetrator programmes work?' – part of the Project Mirabal study that is mentioned within a number of chapters within this book. They knew from previous research that there had been mixed answers to this question, and they believed those mixed findings were due to differing definitions and ways of measuring what was meant by 'what works.' Before starting their investigation into whether such programmes were successful, they first therefore sought to redefine 'success.' They did this by interviewing men on programmes, female partners and ex-partners of men on programmes, funders/commissioners and programme staff. From this, they developed six different measures of success (including respectful communication, freedom as well as safety and shared parenting) which were taken forward into the main part of the evaluation (see Westmarland and Kelly, 2013; Kelly and Westmarland, 2015). This recasting of 'success' beyond the minimal measures of further violence or further police recorded incidents, means that domestic violence perpetrator programmes can be understood and evaluated from a very different perspective.

Listening to women's voices and experiences

What is undeniably at the core of feminist research is the commitment to giving a voice to the marginalised. Hesse-Biber (2012) suggests the central mission of feminist researchers is to conduct research on behalf of women and other oppressed groups with the goal of uncovering subjugated knowledge. As such, the lived experiences of women are prioritised through research which focuses on women as the sources of knowledge (Campbell and Wasco, 2000). As Letherby (2003) states, feminism is both theory and practice. Feminist researchers have a political commitment to produce useful knowledge that will make a difference to women's lives.

Campbell (2002) argues that qualitative methods are best suited to researching rape as they provide opportunities to hear survivors' stories in ways that cannot be matched by quantitative research. The use of interviews and focus groups has a long history in gender, violence and abuse research. This method was favoured by feminist researchers in the 1970s and 1980s who sought to give voice to women who experienced violence and abuse. The way these methods have been used, and continue to be used, is documented in Chapter 4 of this book. Nowadays, technology is enabling interviews and focus groups to be conducted in new ways, opening up opportunities to hear the experiences of women who have previously been less visible in gender, violence and abuse research (for example those living in rural areas, those who do not speak English as a first language or those living in transient environments such as hostels, refuges or refugee camps). Likewise, the recent use of the social media hashtag #metoo represents a powerful example of the ways in which the voices of women around the world are beginning to be 'heard.'

However, listening to women's experiences does not always involve asking them to report their experiences directly to researchers. Other methods that are well suited to listening to women's experiences include ethnography and netnography (internet-based ethnography; see Chapter 9). Similarly, arts-based methods enable researchers to see, and hear, the voices of women through music, dance, poetry, art and photography. These methods are particularly useful for communicating with and 'hearing' women who may not be able to communicate through words, or may prefer to communicate using non-verbal methods.

Incorporating diversity and intersectionality

In 1989 Kimberlé Crenshaw developed the term 'intersectionality' to describe the ways in which different social identities intersect and overlap to create multiple layers of oppression. Specifically, Crenshaw criticised the feminist movement in the 1970s and 1980s which had largely focused on the needs and experiences of white, middle class women (Crenshaw, 1989, 1991). It has been argued that the concept of intersectionality 'is the most important theoretical contribution that women's studies, with related fields, has made so far' (McCall, 2005, p. 1771). Conducting research that captures the experiences of women, men and children from diverse backgrounds in terms of ethnicity, sexuality, (dis)ability, age, class and other social characteristics *should* be a crucial part of the gender, violence and abuse research agenda. The extent to which it *is*, though, is debatable.

In writing this book, we made efforts to ensure that this book encompasses research that takes intersectionality seriously, though it should be acknowledged that at times this was difficult to achieve. There is still a paucity of research that is truly intersectional – and we include some of their own work within this critique. There is an urgent need for diversity to be taken more seriously and to be an integral consideration of funding bids. First steps might include a standalone section within UK Research Council proposals (research bids) that specifies how the proposed research has taken intersectionality into account, and by ensuring that this section is associated with a score which will contribute to the success (or otherwise) of the proposal. This would only be one small intervention though, in what remains a structurally unequal, class based, heteronormative, racist society. Recognising structural racism for what it is, and being more willing to proactively reflect on our practices, is essential (Eddo-Lodge, 2017). We can, and must, do better.

Conducting multidisciplinary and mixed methods research

Beckman (2014) highlights the importance of multidisciplinary and mixed methods research in feminist scholarship. As discussed in the introductory chapter of this book, the debate around whether there is one single feminist research method has now moved on to acceptance that any method can be used in feminist research, so long as it is the right method to address the research questions. This book documents a range of research methods that can be used either as standalone methods or in combination with other methods. This can be inter and intra methodological. For example, Chapter 5 showcases the work of Kanyeredzi's (2014) doctoral research examining African and Caribbean heritage women's experiences of help seeking, and the impact of violence on their relationship to their bodies. Kanyeredzi used a combination of qualitative methods, namely photography, interviews and craft (quilting). Chapter 7 shows how we used both quantitative and qualitative methods to examine sexual violence against older people in the UK (Bows and Westmarland, 2017). Quantitative analysis of police data was used to provide evidence on the extent and nature of sexual violence against people aged 60 and over, whilst interviews with practitioners and older female survivors were used to examine the consequences of sexual violence in later life, service responses to this violence, older women's utilisation of support services and the challenges/barriers to accessing support. In recognition of the importance of multidisciplinary feminist research, Chapter 4 is dedicated to showcasing the ways that researchers work across disciplines and utilise multiple methods to examine different forms of violence and abuse.

Being reflexive

Being reflexive involves the researcher engaging with a continuous reflection of the research process, the data generated and their role in the proceedings. Reflexivity involves the researcher reflecting on their own thoughts and feelings, and, critically, unpacking the causes and influences of these thoughts and feelings. Pio and Singh (2016) stress that this is not narcissism or self-indulgence, but rather a process described by Weick as

> an exercise in disciplined reflexivity. . . . Closer attention to self-as-theorist makes for better theory if that attention is instrumental to spotting excluded voices and if it serves as a data platform for thinking more deeply.
>
> (Weick, 1999, p. 803)

Gilgun describes reflexivity as a connected knowing, 'an approach to understanding that involves the use of self in attempting to be open to the world of others' (Gilgun, 2008, p. 183). Reflexivity also involves being aware of the potential risks of research to the individual researcher, how these risks or harms may affect the research and how researchers themselves can practise resilience. Sampson et al. (2008) note that whilst the emphasis on reflexivity and consideration of power within research relationships is not exclusive to feminist researchers, it has been emphasised and brought to the fore through their writing.

Reflexivity is associated with qualitative methods of research, particularly interviews and ethnography. To this end, there is a growing body of literature discussing reflexivity across multiple domains which draw on qualitative methods, including social work practice and research, nursing, criminology and social science research. As discussed in Chapter 3 of this book, gender, violence and abuse research is often conducted by researchers who also work as practitioners (such as victim advocates or support workers). Carrying out research as both a researcher and a practitioner brings with it a need for ongoing reflexivity. Another example of a situation which requires a high level of reflexivity concerns research conducted by individuals with 'insider/outsider' status, for example police staff who conduct research on policing may find out and have to communicate negative findings to their superior officers, or they may be party to information as police that cannot be used within their research.

One important point that is rarely discussed is positionality as survivor-researchers. Often researchers and victim-survivors as participants are discussed as though there is no overlap between the two. However, in reality there are of course many researchers, policy makers, practitioners and activists who are survivors of violence and abuse but who are not 'out' about their experiences. And nor should they feel they need to be. It is better to remember at all points in the research process that there are still far too many victim-survivors in the world (following on from the problem that there are far too many perpetrators), and that they/we are walking alongside each other, not only as research participants, but also as colleagues, as professionals, as readers of our papers and as audience members at conferences.

Building social relationships in the research process

In addition to hearing the voices of survivors and reducing traditional research power hierarchies, one of the fundamental commitments of feminist research is to conduct research *with women, for women*. Empowering women and involving them as co-producers of knowledge is a priority in feminist research. The techniques used to achieve this have been largely associated with qualitative methods, particularly interviews, focus groups and arts-based methods. These methods allow for dialogue between researcher and participants and provide opportunities for participants to ask their own questions, and to have some control over the information shared and the knowledge produced. In some cases, research designs specifically include participants as co-researchers. This is often referred to as participatory action research (PAR).

In gender, violence and abuse research, involving participants in some or all of the research design and process has significant benefits. Sullivan et al. highlight that, in the case of domestic violence research, involving advocates and survivors 'can be critical to successful and mutually beneficial projects' (Sullivan et al., 2005, p. 978). For example, using a PAR approach enabled Sullivan and colleagues to develop relationships with community members and stakeholders, foster diverse participation and share decision-making, informing the research methods and data analysis. However, participants can be involved in the research process in other ways, for example by examining transcripts of their interviews, attending dissemination events or receiving copies of research reports.

Using research results

The final principle identified by Beckman (2014) is the way research results are used and put into practice. Beckman points out that activism and advocacy 'are at the core of feminist research methodology' (Beckman, 2014, p. 170). Feminist use of research results means more than simply disseminating research findings; rather, it is about the way these findings are used to influence and inform policy, practice and activism. Increasingly, feminist research is seeking to give survivors access to knowledge to help them in their process of recovery, or to help them situate their experiences of the criminal justice system amongst other survivors' experiences. In this sense, the personal really is the political, just as the personal can also be the academic (and vice versa). Indeed, some of the most pressing research agendas arise through a deeply embedded close working relationship with non-academic partners and alongside (other) survivors. Making sure that the research questions being proposed are the right ones to ask, and that the methods and recruitment of participants is realistic, is key to ensuring that the result of research, once completed, are usable. This book dedicates two chapters to exploring the ways feminists have used their research results, including to support activism (Chapter 10), and to inform policy and practice (Chapter 11). Collectively, the chapters within this book highlight the importance of working with grassroots organisations, activists and victim-survivors of abuse to conduct research which generates meaningful data that supports long-term change and facilitates the prevention of violence and abuse.

Summary

Gender, violence and abuse research is guided by the commitments and principles outlined by Beckman (2014). Whilst a range of theoretical and methodological frameworks exist, feminist research is united by this common set of beliefs about how research should be conducted. Each of the chapters in this book examines different methods or approaches to making visible the hidden, and to hearing the voices of those who have been silenced. The book challenges the current orthodoxies for researching and responding to the global problem of violence and abuse – particularly in relation to women and girls but also to a lesser, yet still important, extent in relation to men and boys.

References

Aronson, P. (2017) The dynamics and causes of gender and feminist consciousness and feminist identities, In: H. J. McCammon, V. Taylor, J. Reger and R. L. Einwohner (Eds.) *The Oxford Handbook of Women's Social Movement Activism*. Oxford: Oxford University Press.

Beckman, L. J. (2014) Training in feminist research methodology: Doing research on the margins, *Women & Therapy*, *37*(1–2), pp. 164–177.

Bows, H. and Westmarland, N. (2017) Rape of older people in the United Kingdom: Challenging the 'real-rape' stereotype, *British Journal of Criminology*, *57*(1), pp. 1–17.

Brooks, A. and Hesse-Biber, S. N. (2007) An invitation to feminist research, In: S. N. Hesse-Biber and P. L. Leavy (Eds.) *Feminist Research Practice: A Primer* (pp. 1–26). London: Sage.

Campbell, R. (2002) *Emotionally Involved: The Impact of Researching Rape*. Abingdon: Routledge.

Campbell, R. and Wasco, S. M. (2000) Feminist approaches to social science: Epistemological and methodological tenets, *American Journal of Community Psychology*, *28*(6), pp. 773–791.

Crenshaw, K. (1989) Demarginalizing the intersection of race and sex: A black feminist critique of antidiscrimination doctrine, feminist theory, and antiracist politics, *University of Chicago Legal Forum*, *140*(1), pp. 139–168.

Crenshaw, K. (1991) Mapping the margins: Intersectionality, identity politics, and violence against women of color, *Stanford Law Review*, *43*(6), pp. 1241–1299.

Daly, K. and Chesney-Lind, M. (1988) Feminism and criminology, *Justice Quarterly*, *5*(4), pp. 497–538.

Dickson-Swift, V., James, E. L., Kippen, S. and Liamputtong, P. (2007) Doing sensitive research: What challenges do qualitative researchers face?, *Qualitative Research*, *7*(3), pp. 327–353.

Eddo-Lodge, R. (2017) *Why I'm No Longer Talking to White People about Race*. London: Bloomsbury.

Fontes, L. A. (2004) Ethics in violence against women research: The sensitive, the dangerous, and the overlooked, *Ethics and Behavior*, *14*(2), pp. 141–174.

Gilgun, J. F. (2008) Lived experience, reflexivity, and research on perpetrators of interpersonal violence, *Qualitative Social Work*, *7*(2), pp. 181–197.

Hesse-Biber, S. N. (Ed.) (2012) *Handbook of Feminist Research: Theory and Praxis*, 2nd ed. London: Sage.

Kanyeredzi, A. (2014) *Knowing What I Know Now. Black Women Talk About Violence Inside and Outside of the Home*. PhD Thesis, London: London Metropolitan University. Available at: http://repository.londonmet.ac.uk/679/1/Ava%20Kanyeredzi%20-%20Thesis_Redacted.pdf

Kelly, L. and Westmarland, N. (2015) *Domestic Violence Perpetrator Programmes: Steps towards Change*. Project Mirabal Final Report. London and Durham: London Metropolitan University and Durham University.

Letherby, G. (2003) *Feminist Research in Theory and Practice*. Buckingham: Open University Press.

McCall, L. (2005) The complexity of intersectionality, *Signs: Journal of Women in Culture and Society*, *30*(3), pp. 1771-1800.

Morris, A. and Gelsthorpe, L. (1991) Feminist perspectives in criminology: Transforming and transgressing, *Women & Criminal Justice*, *2*(2), pp. 3-26.

Oakley, A. (1974) *The Sociology of Housework*. London: Martin Robertson.

Oakley, A. (1988) Is social support good for the health of mothers and babies?, *Journal of Reproductive and Infant Psychology*, *6*(1), pp. 3-21.

Office for National Statistics (2018) *Methodology: Improving Crime Statistics for England and Wales - Progress Update July 2018. Latest Update on the Progress Being Made to Improve Crime Statistics for England and Wales*. Available at: https://www.ons.gov.uk/peoplepopulationandcommunity/crimeandjustice/methodologies/improvingcrimestatisticsforenglandandwalesprogressupdate

Pio, E. and Singh, S. (2016) Vulnerability and resilience: Critical reflexivity in gendered violence research, *Third World Quarterly*, *37*(2), pp. 227-244.

Ramazanoglu, C. and Holland, J. (2002) *Feminist Methodology: Challenges and Choices*. London: Sage.

Reinharz, S. and Davidman, L. (1992) *Feminist Methods in Social Research*. Oxford: Oxford University Press.

Rhode, D. L. (1990) Feminist critical theories, *Stanford Law Review*, *42*(3), pp. 617-638.

Robertson, L. and Hale, B. (2011) Interviewing older people: Relationships in qualitative research, *Internet Journal of Allied Health Sciences and Practice*, *9*(3), pp. 1-8.

Sampson, H., Bloor, M. and Fincham, B. (2008) A price worth paying? Considering the cost of reflexive research methods and the influence of feminist ways of doing, *Sociology*, *42*(5), pp. 919-933.

Smart, C. (1995) *Law, Crime and Sexuality: Essays in Feminism*. London: Sage.

Stanley, L. and Wise, S. (2002) *Breaking Out Again: Feminist Ontology and Epistemology*. London: Routledge.

Stark, E. (2007) *Coercive Control: How Men Entrap Women in Personal Life*. New York, NY: Oxford University Press.

Sullivan, M., Bhuyan, R., Senturia, K., Shiu-Thornton, S. and Ciske, S. (2005) Participatory action research in practice: A case study in addressing domestic violence in nine cultural communities, *Journal of Interpersonal Violence*, *20*(8), pp. 977-995.

Tang, N. (2002) Interviewer and interviewee relationships between women, *Sociology*, *36*(3), pp. 703-721.

Weick, K. E. (1999) Theory construction as disciplined reflexivity: Tradeoffs in the 90s, *Academy of Management Review*, *24*(4), pp. 797-806.

Westmarland, N. (2001) The quantitative/qualitative debate and feminist research: A subjective view of objectivity, *Forum: Qualitative Social Research*, *2*(1), Art. 13.

Westmarland, N. and Kelly, N. (2013) Why extending measurements of 'success' in domestic violence perpetrator programmes matters for social work, *British Journal of Social Work*, *43*(6), pp. 1092-1110.

3 Ethical considerations when researching gender, violence and abuse

This chapter provides an introduction to some of the key ethical considerations relating to feminist research. Whilst ethical practice is essential across the broad range of disciplines and methods involved in feminist research, the area of gender, violence and abuse warrants particular consideration. To this end, this chapter examines the approaches taken by violence and abuse researchers to minimise any potential harm to those who participate in their research. It covers some of the current debates around the approaches to ethics in violence against women research, drawing on the recent work by Downes et al. (2014) and others who have problematised blanket assumptions of 'vulnerability' and considered the problems associated with approaches by some research ethics committees. We do not seek to sanitise or simplify this part of the research process, but to demonstrate the complexities involved in this type of research, and to give examples of the ways in which researchers have dealt with some of these issues.

Applying to a research ethics committee

Gaining clearance from a Research Ethics Committee (REC) is an essential component of most research studies. This process is usually fairly straightforward for secondary data analysis of existing data sources, or for research that does not use people directly as research participants (ironically, often dehumanised to 'human or animal subjects' in REC application forms). All RECs have different requirements which can vary over time depending on the perspective taken by the chair/members. At a minimum, most RECs request that researchers provide the following for assessment:

- A completed ethics application form. Blank copies of ethics application forms are typically available from the REC or from the organisation where the research is being carried out (such as a university department or the NHS). The forms vary somewhat according to the nature of the study and the organisation, but they share the common purpose of examining whether the researcher is fully aware of any ethical issues that may arise during their research.

- Draft research tools, for example a questionnaire or interview schedule.
- A copy of the participant information sheet.
- A copy of the 'call for participants' advertisement.
- A copy of the consent form.

In addition to these standard items, violence and abuse researchers may choose to provide a list of resources that can be given to participants at the end of their involvement in the research. For example, in domestic violence research a researcher might make a list that contains: the details of a local domestic violence organisation; the number for a national domestic violence helpline; and contact details for organisations catering for specialist groups such as BAME women, people from the LGBT+ community and men who have experienced domestic violence. Routinely offering this information to individuals who participate in the research is preferable to waiting for them to request it themselves, as they may not feel comfortable asking for the information directly. However, in cases where participants are still living in dangerous situations it is important to ask whether it is safe for them to take such information with them. For example, a participant could be at risk if their partner or ex-partner checks their handbag and discovers the information sheet.

When preparing participant information sheets, it is important to use clear, 'everyday' language and to avoid jargon. This makes it easier for participants to read and understand the information, as well as to provide informed consent. The information sheet should outline the potential risks, but also the potential benefits of taking part in the research. For example, the information sheet may outline how the researcher hopes to use the findings; for many individuals, the knowledge that their experiences (whether positive or negative) could lead to improvements for other people acts as an incentive to engage with the research.

When designing the call for participants, it can be useful for researchers to ask themselves or their friends and family whether they personally would respond to the advertisement. If the response is that they would not, the researcher should seek to make the call more appealing to potential participants. In Project Mirabal (Downes et al., 2014), a study of domestic violence perpetrator programmes (Kelly and Westmarland, 2015), one man explained that he felt motivated to take part in the research because the positive image of a father used on the leaflets given to men demonstrated to him that Project Mirabal might treat perpetrators as fathers and men capable of positive change. He perceived the interviews carried out by Project Mirabal as an opportunity to speak openly about his experiences in a non-judgmental forum and to help other men.

Example: recommendations for ethical decision-making in violence and abuse research

Downes et al. (2014) sought to make visible the ways in which participating in research can be an empowering experience. They argued that research on gender, violence and abuse has been subject to increased ethical scrutiny due to its perception as a 'sensitive' topic involving inherently 'vulnerable' individuals, and that this increased scrutiny has stilted research progress in the field. Paradoxically, excessive ethical scrutiny in this area can lead to greater harm, by limiting the amount of research that is carried out and by making it more difficult for specialist violence and abuse services to demonstrate the effectiveness of their services and approaches. In their Project Mirabal research, Downes et al. (2014) brought together ethical, skilled researchers who were invested in protecting victim-survivors of violence and abuse from further harm whilst also maximising their capacity for self-determination and autonomy. This approach encompassed three core values: conceptualising victim-survivors and perpetrators as active agents; empowering participants to make choices about their lives; and maximising opportunities for positive experiences and impacts of research. Each of these values is discussed in detail below.

Conceptualising victim-survivors and perpetrators as active agents

The women who participated in the research were viewed not as 'passive victims,' but as skillful managers of risk and harm who had the ability to assess whether involvement in research would place themselves or their children at further risk. Women and men were approached as individuals who were able to understand the potential harm, risk and benefits of their participation at numerous points throughout the research process.

Empowering participants to make choices about their own lives

Violence and abuse researchers have a responsibility to support participants who want to make changes in their lives. They should enable opportunities for reflection during the research, and facilitate participant access to local and national support services.

Maximising opportunities for positive experiences and impacts of research

In line with other researchers, such as Campbell et al. (2010), who asked women who had been raped why they decided to take part in research, Downes et al. (2014) found that some women valued the opportunity to 'tell their story' and/ or to gain greater understanding of their experience through the lens of the interview questions. One woman, for example, described how she had decided to take part in the research because she wanted to demonstrate by 'telling her story' how domestic abuse can continue after separation. As Project Mirabal was a longitudinal study, she also found the opportunity to 'track' her own change over time particularly useful. Downes et al. (2014) concluded that it is not just 'empathy' and the interview process that is important but also the content and design of research instruments such as interview schedules and questionnaires.

Based on their work on Project Mirabal, Downes et al. (2014) developed four recommendations for ethical decision-making in violence and abuse research:

1   *To reconsider participants as active agents and stakeholders*. As discussed earlier in this chapter, participants should not be viewed as submissive participants that research 'happens to,' but instead as active agents and stakeholders in the research itself.
2   *To prioritise the development of skilled researchers*. Many of the ethical concerns within violence and abuse research relate to the way research is carried out rather than to the nature of the research itself. By ensuring that researchers possess the necessary training and skills to conduct the research and to manage any ethical issues that may arise, many ethical concerns can be effectively managed as the project progresses. To this end, researchers should be provided with ongoing support, including opportunities to seek advice and to debrief with more experienced researchers.
3   *To develop situated processes of informed consent and confidentiality*. Consent and confidentiality are not static, but rather are fluid and change throughout the research process. Understanding the nature of consent and confidentiality and being realistic with participants about the boundaries of both concepts is critical. Both consent and confidentiality must be assessed on an ongoing basis.
4   *To continue to discuss and share practical experiences of feminist research practice that seeks to deliver justice and social change*. The sharing of best practice amongst feminist researchers is important for the advancement of social justice in a financial and social environment where resources are limited.

Ethical considerations specifically related to gender, violence and abuse research

There are a number of ethical considerations that relate more to violence against women research than to other forms of social research. On the one hand it is important to be able to 'normalise' violence against women research; whilst recruiting individuals who use violence can increase the risk of harm to victim-survivors and to the researchers themselves, it is also important not to 'monstrosize' perpetrators. Most individuals will come into contact with perpetrators of domestic and sexual violence on a daily basis, whether that be at university, at work, in the supermarket, in parent groups or amongst family and friends. Therefore, whilst it is important to draw attention to some of the particular risks and dangers involved in violence against women research, research should not be stilted or stopped because of them. Rather, researchers should speak openly about these risks with the aim of anticipating potential ethical concerns and preparing appropriate responses to any issues that may arise during the course of the research. Indeed, it is often useful to include such discussion when seeking to gain ethical approval for a project from an REC.

Limited/'boundaried' confidentiality

It is important to be accurate about the guarantees that are offered to participants in terms of confidentiality and anonymity. To some extent, this concern is shared with other areas of social research, where it is standard practice to use pseudonyms and to change or omit any features which could be used to identify specific individuals. However, violence and abuse researchers face additional challenges surrounding the issue of confidentiality. It is rarely, if ever, possible to guarantee complete confidentiality and anonymity. Informed consent necessitates that the limits, or boundaries, of confidentiality must be clearly communicated to participants. Some examples of how we have dealt with issues of confidentiality in our own research are described below.

Interviews with practitioners and policy makers

Interviews with members of a domestic violence forum may be identifiable to other members of the forum or to practitioners working alongside that forum. For example, if a quote clearly identified a police perspective and there was consistently one police domestic violence representative within that forum it would be easy for some to link the quote to the individual. This issue cannot be solved simply by removing the link to the organisation, in this instance the police, as research into multi-agency responses relies in part on the situated knowledge of the interviewee. In this situation, being clear with the participant and ensuring that consent is 'informed' means making the participant aware that they may be identified in this way. For example, a participant information sheet might include a passage similar to the following:

> No one taking part will be named in any reports or publications that the research team later produce. However, your job title may be used within publications, which may make you identifiable. You should take this into consideration when deciding whether to take part.

Focus groups with young men about domestic violence awareness programmes

Focus groups bring with them another layer of issues relating to anonymity and confidentiality, as they involve a number of people contributing at the same time. In Stephen Burrell's research with young men (unpublished PhD), he began his sessions with a discussion within the focus group about expectations around not sharing information 'outside the room.' This was included in addition to the informed consent provided individually by each participant. This method of discussing confidentiality relies on a degree of trust with other respondents, and is therefore more suited to groups where participants are talking about their views on a particular topic, rather than their personal experiences of violence and abuse. Nevertheless, the method should not be automatically excluded as a way to approach confidentiality in focus groups concerning experiences of violence. Furthermore, it is important to acknowledge that a disclosure can arise at any time in any research study.

Interviews with victim-survivors and/or perpetrators of violence and abuse

Regardless of whether the participant is a victim-survivor, a perpetrator, a child or even a practitioner, it is possible that the researcher will be told about risks of more violence. In these cases, it is important to specify not only that confidentiality would be limited in these circumstances, but also to be as specific as possible about what would happen under these circumstances. For example in a study with the police in which one of us (Westmarland) was involved which was carried out by the authors, victim-survivor participants were told the following:

> Anything you tell us will be kept confidential unless you tell us something that means that you or another person is at risk of serious harm. In these exceptional circumstances we would inform the police about the risk and

refer you to Harbour support services. We would always inform you if we were planning on doing this and keep you fully informed.

Another project carried out by the authors involved interviews with men who speak out publicly about violence and abuse. In this instance, it was important to be mindful of the possibility that the participants' reasons for speaking out about violence and abuse may have been related to their own personal experiences of these issues. In light of this, participants were provided with the following information:

> We will not use your name within the report, however because of the small number of men who speak out about violence against women it is possible that people who know you well might be able to identify you. Therefore, we are only able to offer limited confidentiality for the main part of the interview. If you tell us personal information that is not otherwise in the public domain such as your own experiences of abuse or as a perpetrator of abuse we will ensure that this part of the interview is fully confidential. Anything you tell us will be kept confidential unless you tell us something that means that you or another person is at risk of serious harm. In these exceptional circumstances, we would inform the police about the risk and refer you to an appropriate support service. We would always inform you if we were planning on doing this and keep you fully informed.

Interviews with convicted perpetrators in prison

As part of research with Marianne Hester looking at the needs of domestic abuse perpetrators, Westmarland interviewed convicted perpetrators, including those serving prison sentences. In those cases the prison requested that they be informed of any previously 'unknown' offences that came to light as part of the interviews. This is a standard clause required of researchers carrying out interviews in prisons, but it has particular implications for researching domestic abuse perpetrators because it is extremely rare that the offence an individual was convicted for will nearly always not have been was a 'one off' incident. Domestic violence and abuse are characterised by ongoing power and control and a high volume of 'incidents' that overlap with each other. In light of this, it would appear that the stipulation to inform the prison of any previously unreported incidents would make it virtually impossible to conduct an interview with a domestic violence perpetrator. However, in reality the prison only required that the information be disclosed in cases where there was enough detail to generate a police report. Therefore, the perpetrators were informed that if they gave the researchers enough information to make a police report viable (e.g. 'I also hit my ex-girlfriend Melissa, who lives next door to my mum on Swan Avenue'), then the disclosure would be passed on to the prison. On the other hand, general information (e.g. 'I have also hit girlfriends in the past, in fact I've been abusive towards most partners') would not be passed on. This allowed participants to make an informed decision about how much information they provided to the researchers.

Potential for research to make the participants' lives worse

It is possible in some cases that involvement in research could put victim-survivors at more risk. As discussed above, steps can be taken to mitigate the physical risk to participants, such as asking each individual if it is safe for them to retain a hard copy of the information sheet. As well as physical safety risks, there is also the possibility that the research process might cause additional emotional distress for participants. This is not a reason to avoid questions that might be seen as 'sensitive' or 'personal,' as for other participants having the opportunity to talk about these issues could be incredibly empowering. Rather, it is important to ensure that the participant genuinely understands that it is acceptable to stop the interview at any point with no detrimental consequences to themselves or others (e.g. in terms of service provision or feeling they are 'letting you down'). Although this information is typically included as a 'tick box' on the consent form, it is important to repeat it, if needed, in a kind and friendly way at relevant points within the interview. Sometimes it can be useful to have a particular content warning for parts of an interview or to specifically repeat the option of not answering individual questions whilst still participating in the research as a whole. For example, the research team working on Project Mirabal took part in a number of discussions about whether to ask women victim-survivors whether or not they had been raped by their partner or ex-partner. These discussions were particularly important given that one of the four researchers carrying out the telephone interviews was a man, and discussing sexual assault with a man could have been additionally distressing for women victim-survivors of male violence. It was decided that the question would be included in the interviews because not to ask would be to sideline sexual violence within research about domestic violence. However, it was decided that the question would be prefaced with the following reminder:

> The next question is about sexual behaviour. I would like to remind you that all answers are confidential and you don't have to answer questions you don't wish to.

In addition, it was decided that the terms 'rape' and 'sexual violence' would not be used, with the interviewers instead asking participants if someone 'made you do something sexual you did not want to do.' This decision was made in light of the fact that some victim-survivors are not in a position where they acknowledge the acts against them as rape or sexual violence.

One way that the research process can have the potential to make the lives of victims worse is how the researcher acts and responds to the participant during the interview. Whilst it is perhaps obvious that a kind and caring manner should be taken whilst interviewing victim-survivors, the manner in which a feminist researcher should approach a perpetrator of violence is less clear. It is important to respect the perpetrator's participation in the research, to ensure he has access to the same ethical standards as other participants, and also to ensure that the research process is not distressing. The interview process should not be a shaming process; indeed, many perpetrators already feel some element of shame about their use of violence and abuse. However, it is also important that the researcher does not tacitly condone violence and abuse. For example, 'prompts' and non-verbal communication that are commonly used within interviews to make participants feel comfortable (e.g. nodding head, saying things such as 'yes I understand') need to be considered in context when interviewing perpetrators. As with interviews with victim-survivors, the gender of the interviewer can also affect the outcome of the process. In Project Mirabal Westmarland and her colleagues their colleagues worked with one of their partner organisations (Respect) to role play interviews with perpetrators. This allowed the researchers to practice how they might respond to different circumstances. For example, in one role play exercise the (male) interviewer had to respond to a perpetrator who was asking him to agree that he 'knew what women could be like.'

Potential dangers for researchers

In addition to the safety of the participants, the safety of those conducting the research is also likely to be one of the primary considerations of an ethics committee. The nature of the risk to researchers, as well as the steps that could be taken to reduce this risk, depend on a wide range of factors that are specific to different research studies and contexts. There is an obvious heightening of risk if interviews are going to be conducted in people's homes or other private spaces. Common mitigations for this include not interviewing perpetrators in their own homes, not interviewing victim-survivors at home if there is any likelihood of being interrupted by the perpetrator, and having a safety protocol which includes 'checking in' with either the lead investigator or the project administrator at the start and at the end of an interview. This 'checking in' helps to protect the researcher as it ensures that the project administrator is aware of when and where the interview is being conducted.

Researchers are increasingly using social media channels such as Twitter and Facebook at different stages in the research process – including recruitment of participants and dissemination of findings. This brings with it great positive opportunities for academic engagement with the wider public. However, it also brings with it the potential for online 'trolling.' The term 'trolling' refers to abusive online behaviour which is often (but not always) written by anonymous individuals and can range from name-calling to threats of rape and violence. Whilst trolling can happen to any researcher, it occurs more commonly in response to work or writing on specific topics, one of which is (ironically) the topic of violence against women. Lewis et al. (2016) looked at this topic from the perspective of those receiving the online abuse. They argue that online abuse of feminists is in itself a form of violence against women, with Twitter being the most common site for abusive communications. They carried out a survey and interviews with women who spoke out online about feminist issues (including but not solely on the issue of violence against women). In total, 40 percent of their survey respondents had been sexually harassed and 37 percent experienced threats of sexual violence, including rape threats, online. Not surprisingly, given the sexually violent nature of the threats, much of the abuse had clear links to the upholding of patriarchal privileges:

> I was Tweeting about #EverydaySexism and received emails from several men detailing how they were going to sexually abuse me to remind me who was in control in society.
>
> (Respondent 103 in Lewis et al., 2016, p. 1471)

Although this project was not focused on the experiences of researchers, it is highly relevant given that researchers are increasingly being encouraged to use online platforms to disseminate their findings and increase public engagement with their work.

Ethical partnership working

An area that has received less academic attention concerns the importance of maintaining respectful and ethical working relationships with any organisations that may be involved in the research. This is important when working with any organisations that are (official or unofficial) partners in research generally, but is arguably particularly important in terms of women's sector voluntary and community organisations which may be especially challenged from a resources perspective. An ongoing reflection on the relatively privileged position of academic researchers and of the competing demands experienced by non-academic organisations, particularly those providing direct services to victim-survivors, is crucial. To a researcher, the success of their research project is probably their primary work-based consideration and is always at the top of their 'to do list.' For an organisation dealing with funding difficulties, managing overworked staff and volunteers, supporting clients in crisis and/or with longer term support needs and managing safety and risk for staff and clients, research is often at the bottom of their 'to do list.' In some cases it is not even on their list. This could be because of the competing pressures, because they do not see engaging with researchers as having any benefit to their organisation, or because they have previously had negative experiences of research partnerships. Sometimes organisations can feel 'over researched,' especially when the type of work they do is under the spotlight due to research funding priorities or media interest.

It is also important that researchers do not expect a non-academic organisation to 'educate' them. To gain positive responses and maintain ongoing partnerships, researchers should approach organisations with the intention of giving back at least the same amount as they are 'taking' from the organisation. For example, in a case where a researcher asks an organisation to put up project recruitment posters in their offices, the researcher should as a minimum offer to print out the posters and send them to the organisation's offices. Ideally, the researcher should offer something additional in return, for example by spreading the word if the organisation is looking for new trustees, or by offering to help find academic research to support them in any funding bids they might be preparing.

In cases where researchers are listing an organisation as a place that participants can access for support needs, it is important that they consider the resource implications of this for the organisation itself. If it is a small, local organisation the researcher should ensure that the organisation is happy to be listed as a resource for participants. If it is a larger national organisation, such as a national domestic violence helpline, then this is less of an immediate consideration, but the researcher might still consider how they might 'give something back,' for example by doing a sponsored run or a cake bake in aid of the charity.

Data management

There are certain data protection requirements that all researchers must follow by law. In the UK and other European Union countries these are set out within the General Data Protection Regulation. However, there are also specific additional issues regarding the management of data collected by violence and abuse researchers, particularly around the archiving of data. The UK data service is a collection of social, economic and population data which is funded by the Economic and Social Research Council (ESRC). It provides quantitative, qualitative and mixed methods data for secondary analysis by researchers, and spans many disciplines and themes. Many grant application forms will ask applicants to state whether they will be archiving their data via this UK data service. Applicants who do not wish to archive their data are asked by the ESRC to provide an explanation for this choice.

Researchers within the field of violence and abuse have taken different approaches to the issue of archiving data. In Donovan and Hester's (2009) ESRC study 'Comparing Love and Domestic Violence in Heterosexual and Same Sex Relationships, 2005-2006,' the authors decided to archive both the survey data and the interview data but not the focus group data. A search for 'domestic violence' (conducted April 2018) in the UK data service archive produces 921 results for variables and questions from survey data sets, with many of the results from surveys such as British Crime Surveys and police attitudes surveys. It is typically more straightforward to anonymise quantitative data than qualitative data. However, it is still possible to archive qualitative and mixed methods data, as long as the level of anonymisation is high enough. In Project Mirabal, Kelly and Westmarland decided not to archive the data, giving reasons that were accepted by the ESRC (that the level of anonymisation needed would be such that the data would not be useful, and that perpetrators who took part in the study as participants could pose as researchers to find 'their victim's' data). Participants should be given the choice whether to consent to participate in the study only, or to consent to both participation in the study and the archiving of their data. Beyond this, there is no blanket 'rule' about archiving data, and decisions should be made on a project by project basis.

Summary

This chapter has outlined some of the key ethical considerations in violence against women research. Whilst most, if not all, research carries ethical risks and concerns that must be identified and mitigated wherever possible, violence against women research produces a number of specific considerations, some of which have been discussed here. Broadly, these ethical concerns relate to the subject area (one which is often deemed to be sensitive and involving vulnerable participants, although the use of terms such as 'sensitive' and 'vulnerable' in this context are questionable) and the methods employed. However, shown in this chapter, these ethical concerns are generally not insurmountable and should not prevent the critical research that is needed in this area.

References

Campbell, R., Adams, A. E., Wasco, S. M., Ahrens, C. E. and Sefl, T. (2010) 'What has it been like for you to talk with me today?' The impact of participating in interview research on rape survivors, *Violence against Women*, 16(1), pp. 60–83.

Donovan, C. and Hester, M. (2009) *Comparing Love and Domestic Violence in Heterosexual and Same Sex Relationships, 2005-2006* [data collection]. UK Data Service, Accessed 27 April 2018, SN: 6332, DOI: 10.5255/UKDA-SN-6332-1.

Downes, J., Kelly, L. and Westmarland, N. (2014) Ethics in violence and abuse research: A positive empowerment approach, *Sociological Research Online*, 19(1), pp. 1–13.

Kelly, L. and Westmarland, N. (2015) *Domestic Violence Perpetrator Programmes: Steps towards Change*. Project Mirabal Final Report. London and Durham: London Metropolitan University and Durham University.

Lewis, R., Rowe, M. and Wiper, C. (2016) Online abuse of feminists as an emerging form of violence against women and girls, *British Journal of Criminology*, 57(6), pp. 1462–1481.

4 Multidisciplinary and partnership working

This chapter focuses on working with others both inside and outside academia to design, conduct and disseminate research. First, the chapter describes how research on gender, violence and abuse cuts across different academic disciplines including sociology, psychology, criminology, law, anthropology, health and medicine. It then considers the challenges and opportunities that associated with working across disciplinary boundaries. Next, the chapter describes how feminist research on gender, violence and abuse has been conducted in partnership with non-academic collaborators, using a historical overview of feminist academics working with the police as an example.

Multidisciplinary research on gender, violence and abuse

The study of gender, violence and abuse is inherently multidisciplinary in nature. As such, it is impossible to pinpoint a 'home' discipline for such research, although its origins are arguably most rooted in sociology (and more specifically in feminist or women's studies). Many of the key academic journals in this field echo the multidisciplinary nature of the topic, with journals such as Sage's 'Violence Against Women' and 'Journal of Interpersonal Violence' and Policy Press's more recently launched 'Journal of Gender Based Violence' all emphasising the multidisciplinary make-up of their readerships. 'Violence Against Women,' for example, describes itself as 'an international, interdisciplinary journal dedicated to the publication of research and information on all aspects of the problem of violence against women.' Similarly, the 'Journal of Gender Based Violence' states that it is the first international journal based in Europe to show case the work of scholars across disciplinary and topic boundaries, and from a range of methodologies.

(www.policypress.co.uk/journals/journal-of-gender-based-violence)

Below are listed other key disciplines with examples of studies conducted from these approaches, although it must be noted that there are many overlaps and fuzzy boundaries to each of these disciplines:

- *Sociology* – broadly, sociology can be conceptualised as the study of human society. It is often considered the umbrella discipline also for feminist/women's studies and anti-racism studies, though these fields also draw strongly upon other disciplines, such as criminology. Examples of research that falls under the heading of sociology include: the media's portrayal of rape victim-survivors, sexism and racism within music videos, theories of masculinities as they relate to perpetrators of domestic abuse and how disability affects women's experiences of trying to leave domestic violence.
- *Criminology* – this discipline overlaps strongly with sociology and law and includes topics such as policing domestic abuse, rape and the criminal justice system, why men use violence and abuse, the way the criminal justice system deals with domestic and sexual violence, whether domestic abuse perpetrator programmes 'work' and the effectiveness of criminal justice interventions on reducing violence and abuse.
- *Law* – research within this field is closely related to criminological research, especially in its sub field of socio-legal studies. Legal research on gender, violence and abuse includes: work on the domestic and international legal regulation of different forms of violence and abuse, theorising justice, investigation of issues relating to the judiciary, examination of the human rights dimensions of abuse and assessment of the effectiveness of different legal systems.
- *Anthropology* – this discipline is concerned with the study of culture and society. Anthropological research on gender, violence and abuse seeks to develop in-depth understandings about harmful cultural practices such as child brides, female genital mutilation, so called 'honour' based violence and the experiences of women seeking help from different cultural backgrounds.
- *Education* – gender, violence and abuse research within the field of education addresses topics such as the role and effectiveness of sex and relationship workshops in schools, the nature and extent of sexual violence in higher education and the usefulness of intervention programmes designed to prevent violence and abuse in higher education.

- *Health and medicine* – work within these fields includes research on the health, mental health and well-being impacts of violence and abuse; the development of best practice in forensic medical examinations for rape survivors; the identification of women in maternity services who are experiencing domestic or sexual violence; and the healthcare needs of women who have experienced female genital mutilation.
- *Psychology* – this field concerns the study of the brain and behaviour. Psychology overlaps with sociology and with health and medicine, and includes some large-scale attitudinal studies for example on 'rape myths.' Other research within this field concerns the assessment of different forms of counselling for victim-survivors, psychometric testing of sex offenders and examination of the effects of sexual abuse on the brain.
- *Social policy* – research within this field includes examination of the ways in which different policy initiatives seek to reduce gender, violence and abuse; how wider changes to the welfare system impact women, especially those experiencing violence and abuse; and how government policies are applied differentially to different groups of women.
- *Social work* – researchers in this field study topics such as: how to work with young people who display sexually abusive behaviours, child protection and domestic violence, how to support young people at risk of sexual exploitation and the improvement of social work policies and practices concerning responses to domestic violence perpetrators.
- *Human geography* – this field covers a range of topics related to gender, violence and abuse, including how space and place interact with different forms of violence and abuse, the ways in which the physical and social environments shape and influence the perpetration of violence and abuse, embodied experiences of victim-survivors, social and cultural relations, the role of communities and cultures in the maintenance or prevention of violence and abuse and the influence of geopolitical factors on gendered violence.
- *International relations* – also known as international studies, this field examines global connections within politics, economics and law. Researchers studying gender, violence and abuse from an international relations perspective focus on topics such as the role of natural disasters on rates of violence and abuse, the ways in which wars and conflicts impact on rates of rape and sexual violence and the difficulties in providing interventions in these contexts and access to sexual healthcare for girls and women in remote parts of the world.
- *Politics* – research within the discipline of politics has addressed topics such as trafficking for the purposes of sexual exploitation; the issue of prostitution; the role of the state with regards to femicide; how gender, violence

and abuse is linked to political violence and conflict situations such as 'the troubles' in Northern Ireland; and the role of international organisations, such as the UN, in addressing gendered violence.

The aim of this lengthy (yet simultaneously limited) list of disciplines is to illustrate the breadth of areas within which gender, violence and abuse research can be conducted. This work is often carried out at and across disciplinary boundaries. The following section considers some of the challenges that can occur when researchers from different fields and methodological backgrounds work together to study gender, violence and abuse.

Challenges of multidisciplinary working

Whilst a multidisciplinary approach can enrich research and provide a more nuanced discussion of a topic, it nevertheless brings with it a number of barriers and challenges.

There can be great variation across disciplines in terms of methodological approach and research methods employed. Similarly, researchers from different disciplines can disagree on the best approach to take when seeking a sound basis for research excellence, assessing the validity of findings and advancing theory. For example, appropriate sample sizes, sampling techniques and the language used when reporting findings can vary between research fields.

Despite studying the same topic, two gender, violence and abuse researchers can be surprisingly far away from one another in terms of their methodological approach. This can make the process of carrying out the research much more stressful and time consuming.

There is surprisingly little written about the advantages and disadvantages of conducting multidisciplinary research; in the few cases where it is addressed, it is usually assumed to be a positive development. This optimism can lead to a lack of attention being paid to the challenges that may be experienced (and how these challenges might be overcome). Newell and Galliers (2000), for example, argue that it is important to recognise that conflict is likely when people from different backgrounds join research teams, and that such conflict needs to be acknowledged and confronted.

In 2009, Jordan highlighted that violence against women research is a relatively young field of study. Although Jordan was writing a decade ago and there has been significant development since then, the challenges she identified are still valid today. She argues that the lack of one disciplinary home limits the identification, cohesiveness and maturation of violence against women researchers.

This, she points out, also limits the ability to meet at conferences as the major associations organise their conferences around disciplinary boundaries. The multidisciplinary nature of the field also means that there is no single route to becoming an accredited violence against women researcher. Acknowledging that her ideas might be controversial, she argues that violence against women research should move away from 'research agendas,' which cannot account for the complexities of the issue, and make a claim to be an area of science, as successfully argued by researchers in the field of psychology during the mid-1900s. In her words,

> Use of the word *science*, then, is valid to the extent that the application is to an organised body of knowledge, a methodologically sound approach to its study, and an organised group of scientists. The application here is not an attempt to elevate the study of VAW [violence against women] to the same footing as the natural sciences; rather, it is an effort to extend to the field the advantages that organisation as a science would bring.
>
> (Jordan, 2009, p. 18)

This, she argues, would offer both pragmatic and theoretical benefits, improving organisation of knowledge, establishing a structure for testing and retesting theories and providing theoretical constructs that are associated with researchers in the field – something she argues would give clarity to the fundamental principles that guide the field. This, Jordan suggests, would move violence against women research to a paradigmatic rather than a descriptive science.

Opportunities brought about by multidisciplinary working

In the section above, Jordan (2009) makes some very valid and important claims about the challenges that violence against women research faces as a result of the number of disciplines it is required to work across. However, she advocates for the positioning of violence against women research as a transdisciplinary science, rather than bringing it all into one discipline. Indeed, there are many opportunities generated by multidisciplinary working that might not arise if violence against women researchers were all to work within one single field (although Jordan does conceive it as a transdisciplinary science).

One opportunity has clear benefits in terms of the purpose of this book more broadly – the ability to use the most appropriate research methods to answer the research question(s) a project is seeking to answer. The term 'innovative methods' is used relatively frequently within funding bids and sometimes articles, but what is innovative within one discipline can be standard practice in another. Multidisciplinary research allows for the application of expertise from one field to answer a question in a different field. Therefore, it is able to facilitate innovative research which does not depend on the development of entirely new methods or paradigms. For example, as Chapter 7 shows, arts-based and creative methods research is fairly 'new' in social sciences and is viewed as an innovative approach, yet it has a rich history in the humanities. Similarly, the ethnographic work in Chapter 9 is unusual and therefore 'innovative' in some disciplines, yet represents a standard method within anthropology.

Working in multidisciplinary teams might have particular benefits for the development of theory, for example a multidisciplinary partnership could enable a particular theoretical leap to be made. Hence, there is the potential for particularly transformative work to be carried out within such teams:

> Unexpected yet fascinating results and greater theoretical insights can emerge when researchers are empathetic to and knowledgeable of the interests and objectives of other stakeholders. Thus, rather than viewing requirements of other team members as potential constraints, it is worthwhile to leverage these different perspectives to achieve greater theoretically significant outcomes arising from the synergistic activities of multidisciplinary research.
>
> (Cuevas et al., 2012, p. 63)

This may well be the primary reason why research funders and many researchers see, on balance, more advantages than disadvantages to multidisciplinary research, and why so many academics are willing to try to work through the challenges.

Partnership working with non-academics

As well as working with academics in other disciplines, working with non-academics in organisations is also key for many successful research projects. This is particularly important given the increased emphasis on creating 'real world impact,' something that many funding bodies now require. Under the UK higher education funding system the Research Excellence Framework (REF), units of assessment (that map broadly onto disciplines) are required to demonstrate the impact of their research and funding is allocated according to excellence within this. Although it is possible to conduct research without non-academic partners and then work with partners at the dissemination stage, it is generally accepted that to 'build in' impact from the start means working with partners in a more holistic, longer term way. This brings with it particular challenges and opportunities, some of which overlap with those identified already in this chapter but others that are more distinct.

The organisations and individuals that academics working on gender, violence and abuse research have tended to work with in the UK include: the police, prisons, probation services, doctors' surgeries, hospitals, midwifery units, social workers, children's workers, youth workers, Women's Aid, Rape Crisis Centres, Black women's organisations, women's centres, children's centres and schools. Despite the extent of this partnership working, there has been scant academic research into how such partnerships have developed over the four decades that gender, violence and abuse research has been conducted. One area in which partnership working raises a number of political and professional challenges for both parties is the policing of domestic violence and abuse. This is discussed in the example below. Policing has been chosen as it is arguably the setting in which partnership working has come, if not the furthest, then at least a considerable distance. Furthermore, although tensions do arise, this partnership is seemingly essential to the goal of improving experiences for victims, and is therefore particularly worthy of further discussion.

Example: police and academics working together to end domestic violence and abuse

Partnerships between academics and police forces are commonplace, with participatory and action research thought to be particularly useful methods of collaboration between these two parties (Murji, 2010). These research methods emphasise the process of working together to effect change within an organisation. Given that the process will therefore be somewhat specific to those engaged within it, it has been argued that 'off-the-shelf' guides on collaboration may be limited in what they can achieve (Murji, 2010). However, it is has been suggested that productive working relationships are typically underpinned by characteristics such as continuous communication, negotiation and the ability to understand the perspective of the other party (Fleming, 2010). As such, research of this nature should seek to embody these characteristics.

Police and academic partnerships in the area of gender, violence and abuse have developed over time. In the UK, this partnership working has undergone four broad phases. Phase One, lasting from the 1960s until approximately 1990, was characterised by minimal engagement, some animosity, little understanding and the absence of any desire from feminist academics or police to work together. Often, feminist academics were also activists who were critical of the police response to violence against women and did not view police as potential research partners. In a small number of cases, academics were able to conduct interviews with the police as part of a wider project – most notably Hanmer's project in West Yorkshire which used research interviews to document police officers' views on policing domestic violence and child sexual abuse. It is likely that West Yorkshire was particularly ahead of its time in terms of its highly active women's movement, Women's Aid groups and Rape Crisis Centres. The strength of the West Yorkshire women's movement was linked in part to the West Yorkshire police's response to women during the Peter Sutcliffe investigation, feminist activists' highly visible anti-pornography actions in the region and the domestic violence murder of a woman in Bradford (West Yorkshire) where the police were criticised nationally. Hanmer's research was therefore unusual, taking place under a specific set of circumstances, and was undoubtedly only made possible through extensive negotiations and a high level of trust between the researcher and the police.

Phase Two of partnership working within this field lasted around a decade, from 1990 until 2000. It was characterised by an acceptance by the police and government organisations that academic research was needed in order to improve their responses to domestic violence and rape (other forms of gendered violence and abuse were largely overlooked). Acceptance of the widespread and serious nature of violence and abuse against women was beginning to increase, and there were an increasing number of women speaking out about poor practice by the police and judges in particular, but also other parts of the criminal justice system. In this time, the police and government organisations did not have a strong enough relationship with feminist academics to work with or commission them to conduct this research. Instead they used their own researchers to produce reports which went on to be highly influential not only in policing/governmental terms but also within academia. Some key examples of this type of work are Kelly et al.'s (1999) study 'Domestic Violence Matters' – a project in London where civilian crisis counsellors were placed in two police stations to offer an out of hours service to victims at the time they needed it – and Mirrlees-Black (1999) analysis of the British Crime Survey (now known as the Crime Survey for England and Wales, discussed later in Chapter 6). In this phase, therefore, research was beginning to be deemed important, but the partnership working in research terms was not yet well developed. Where it did exist, it tended to be mediated in some way by the Home Office or Scottish Office, typically as part of a broader policy approach funded by central government. Academics, however, were very influential in the multi-agency fora that were starting to spread across the UK in the 1990s. At the time these fora were largely led by voluntary sector women's groups and local activists. The police were also invited to these groups, and relationships started to grow during the latter stages of this period.

Phase Three, which lasted from approximately 2000 until the early 2010s, saw a huge increase in the level of gender, violence and abuse research that was conducted by academics working from a criminological and policing perspective. It was during this phase that the ESRC Violence initiative (1999–2002) was introduced. This initiative was a £500,000 programme of research led by Professor Betsy Stanko. It was designed to expand and enhance understanding of different forms of violence against the person, with an aim to facilitate the prevention, reduction or elimination of such violence. Whilst Stanko, a long-standing feminist academic specialising in policing and domestic violence, led the research, the programme also had a large number of workshops and individual research projects associated with it. This phase also saw the enactment of the New Labour Plans to develop a new, evidence-based approach to 'tackle' different forms of crime in the most cost-effective way possible – this was called the Crime Reduction Programme (1999–2002). Within this was the Violence against Women Initiative, led by Programme Director Alana Diamond, which aimed to 'identify the most appropriate and cost-effective approaches to reducing domestic violence, rape and sexual assault by known perpetrators' (Diamond, 2000, p. 16). The Crime Reduction Programme also contained a stream of work on prostitution and commercial sexual exploitation yet this, controversially, was not contained under the heading of the Violence against Women Initiative. The programme was originally conceived as research driven, with a level of funding for interventions and evaluations which was unprecedented in the UK criminology field (Maguire, 2004). However, it suffered from a number of problems and ultimately failed to deliver on what many saw as an overly ambitious programme of work (Maguire, 2004).

Phase Four, lasting from the early 2010s until the present day, has seen police and academics working closer together in a more partnership-focused approach than a 'researcher/researched' position. The co-production of knowledge and partnership working has become generally more promoted within research, which has had an impact on the way that research is designed and the methods that are used. Police are now far more involved in the design of research, and in many cases are far more transparent and open to researchers, including in areas where they may face criticism. A key example of this is the N8 Policing Research Partnership, which has at its very core the development of sustainable partnerships between academics and policing partners. Its stated aims are to 'enable and foster research collaborations that will help address the problems of policing in the 21st century and achieve international excellence in policing research' (N8 Policing Research Partnership, www.n8prp.org.uk). Its objectives include transforming the ways in which researchers engage with policing partners in research co-production, fostering knowledge exchange internationally, sharing data and exploiting data analytics and pioneering a model for sustainable collaborations. At the request of the policing partners, domestic abuse has become a key priority for the N8 Partnership, and there are a number of projects running which have both police and academics as investigators, including some 'staff exchange' projects where academics spend time within the police or police spend time working as an academic.

Clearly, there has been a long journey in terms of how academics and the police have worked together to develop gender, violence and abuse research. In many ways, the journey outlined above echoes a general pattern of change in how applied research, action research and research with policy and practice implications are carried out. There now exists a much more impact-driven, ethical, partnership-based approach to doing research, and this has resulted in positive developments in police/academic research partnerships.

Summary

This chapter has provided a brief overview of some of the issues involved in doing research with academic partners from different disciplines, and with non-academic partners such as the police. These relationships may not be easy, and it is important to be aware of potential challenges so that they can be addressed as part of the research process. Where these challenges can be overcome, such partnerships have the potential to drive theoretical and methodological developments that might not be possible with less collaborative approaches.

References

Cuevas, H. M., Bolstad, C. A., Oberbreckling, R., LaVoie, N., Mitchell, D. K., Fielder, J. and Foltz, P. W. (2012) Benefits and challenges of multidisciplinary project teams: 'Lessons learned' for researchers and practitioners, *ITEA Journal of Test & Evaluation*, *33*(1), pp. 58–65.

Diamond, A. (2000) Violence against women: The Crime Reduction Programme initiative, *Criminal Justice Matters*, *42*(1), pp. 16–17.

Fleming, J. (2010) Learning to work together: Police and academics, *Policing: A Journal of Policy and Practice*, *4*(2), pp. 139–145.

Jordan, C. E. (2009) Advancing the study of violence against women: Evolving research agendas into science, *Violence against Women*, *15*(4), pp. 393–419.

Kelly, L., Bindel, J., Burton, B., Butterworth, D., Cook, K. and Regan, L. (1999) *Domestic Violence Matters: An Evaluation of a Development Project*. Home Office Research Study 193. London: Home Office.

Maguire, M. (2004) The Crime Reduction Programme in England and Wales: Reflections on the vision and the reality, *Criminology & Criminal Justice*, *4*(3), pp. 213–237.

Mirrlees-Black, C. (1999) *Domestic Violence: Findings from a New British Crime Survey Self-Completion Questionnaire*. Home Office Research Study 191. London: Home Office.

Murji, K. (2010) Introduction: Academic-Police collaborations: Beyond 'two worlds', *Policing: A Journal of Policy and Practice*, 4(2), pp. 92–94.

Newell, S. and Galliers, R. D. (2000) More than a footnote: The perils of multidisciplinary research collaboration, *AMCIS 2000 Proceedings*, *304*, pp. 1738–1742.

PART II

Research methods

5 Interviews and focus groups

Qualitative interviews and focus groups have long been popular methods amongst feminist researchers. This chapter considers the ways in which interviews and focus groups have been used in such research, focusing specifically on the use of these methods in work on violence and abuse. The chapter begins by addressing the practical issues that can arise during interviews and focus groups. To this end, the chapter addresses an example of how the semi-structured interview was used by one of the authors (Bows) to interview older women who had been raped. This is followed by a discussion of the practical considerations around conducting semi-structured interviews, including ways to open and close interviews, and the design of interview guides. The chapter then addresses focus groups, considering the problems associated with 'big' voices within focus group, something which is exemplified by work carried out by one of the authors (Westmarland). Next, the chapter considers the role of the research interviewer themselves, focusing on an example of a project where the interviewer (Coy) had to manage different roles as a research interviewer and as a support worker, and the challenges and opportunities that this dual role brought. The chapter then goes on to discuss the impact of research interviews on participants, researchers and transcribers. Whilst most of the chapter focuses on victim-survivors of violence and abuse as research participants, the last part of the chapter turns to the issues involved in carrying out feminist research with men who have used violence and abuse, a topic which raises particular concern amongst feminist writers.

Types of interviews and focus groups

Corbin and Morse (2003) identify several types of interviews: unstructured interactive interviews, semi-structured interviews and structured interviews. The main difference between these types of interview concerns the degree to which participants have control over the process and content of the interview (Fontana and Frey, 1994; Morse, 2002). Structured interviews usually consist of closed questions with an exhaustive list of potential responses (overlapping with survey research), whereas unstructured interviews contain fewer questions and are very open in style (Rubin and Rubin, 1995). As discussed in Chapter 1, interviews have been one of the most common methods in gender, violence and abuse research. Interview methods have a long history in research examining domestic violence and sexual violence but are also utilised in research addressing under-explored forms of violence including honour-based violence (Gill et al., 2012), forced married (Chantler et al., 2009), female genital mutilation (Gangoli et al., 2018), and, recently, they have been used to examine the experiences of male and female acid-violence survivors (Khoshnami et al., 2017). In the latter study, interviews were particularly useful as so little evidence is currently available on the extent, causes and consequences of acid-violence. The researchers were able to use interviews with 12 survivors to develop a conceptual model to explain causal conditions, intervening conditions, context, action/interactional strategies and consequences of acid-violence. Similarly, in the first national study to examine domestic violence against disabled women, Hague et al. (2011) conducted in-depth interviews with survivors to investigate experiences of abuse and help seeking combined with surveys of practitioners in domestic support organisations and disability services to explore service provision, barriers and challenges to accessing support.

The style of interview adopted depends on the aims of the research. For example, where very little is known about a particular topic or issue, unstructured interviews or focus groups may offer the best approach as they provide greater space for issues to be raised. Where more is known about a topic and the purpose of the research is to explore a particular aspect of this topic (e.g. how the police investigate same-sex domestic violence), more structured questions may be appropriate to ensure the data gathered specifically relates to the key areas the research seeks to explore.

As with interviews, focus groups can be more or less structured, with differing levels of researcher facilitation. This depends in part on the personality and skills of the researcher, but also on the group dynamics, for example whether group members already know each other or have come together solely for the purpose of the research, or whether there are 'big' voices that dominate the group.

Example: using semi-structured interviews to interview older women who have been raped

Semi-structured interviews are the most frequently used form of interview within feminist research. Within this category of interview there is room for 'more' or 'less' structure, and space for more innovative or unusual styles of interviewing. The term 'semi-structured' is often used synonymously with the term 'in-depth,' and either might be used to describe this kind of interview. One of the authors (Bows) chose to use semi-structured interviews as part of a larger doctoral study (supervised by Westmarland) examining older women's recent experiences of rape and sexual violence. Three qualitative, semi-structured interviews with older women survivors of sexual violence were conducted to explore their experiences. Although research on older women and domestic abuse existed at the time of the research, no previous studies had included the stories or individual experiences of older women who had experienced sexual violence in later life. As so little is known about violence experienced by older women in later life, semi-structured interviews were chosen as they allowed for a structured discussion to answer the PhD research questions, but provided room for participants to shape the nature and direction of the broader discussion. This meant there was space in the interviews for the researcher to understand participants' 'ideas, thoughts and memories in their own words, rather than the words of the researcher' (Reinharz and Davidman, 1992, p. 19).

The interview schedule was intentionally broad, with open questions covering the consequences of sexual violence for older women, reporting/disclosure decisions, experiences of support agencies and challenges/barriers in accessing support. Minocha et al. (2013) suggest that older women may prefer an open conversation approach, as opposed to structured interview methods. With this in mind, and to build rapport, the interviews began with 'small talk'; the first section asked the survivor about themselves, whether they had lived in the local area for a long time and whether they had children/grandchildren. The interview then moved on to asking the interviewees how they had come to be involved in the support service through which they had been invited to participate in the research.

When so little is known about a particular topic, as in this research, semi-structured interviews are useful as they ensure certain questions are asked which address the overall research questions, but allow flexibility to explore broader issues which, given the lack of previous knowledge, would be difficult to gather using quantitative methods or structured interviews. For example, in all three interviews the women spoke about previous experiences of sexual violence earlier in their life, despite the fact that none of the interview questions asked about this. The flexibility of the semi-structured interview allowed the researcher to ask questions about the participants' perceptions and feelings in relation to both previous and recent experiences of sexual violence. It should be noted that this approach did lead to the interviews being highly varied in terms of their duration (in this case between one and four hours), given that they were largely guided by how much the survivor wanted to talk.

Example: using focus groups to explore how young men understand and use domestic violence prevention campaigns

In his PhD research, Burrell (2018; supervised by Westmarland) conducted eight focus groups with men's sports teams at a university. He chose focus groups as his method because of their ability to examine group interactions and to facilitate the shared production of meaning. His focus groups were loosely structured and based around the presentation of several short prevention campaign videos. Taking the attention away from themselves and their own experiences or perpetration of domestic violence allowed the men to talk instead about how effective they thought the campaign videos would be for young men like themselves. Burrell (2018) found that the videos provided an external focus for the discussion which allowed the men to discuss partner violence in a way that did not rely on internal experiences, knowledge and understanding. This allowed participants to approach the discussion without finding themselves in a personally vulnerable position. However, Burrell recognised that even by asking questions about interpersonal violence he was asking a lot from his participants – that they discuss an issue that is not seen as a 'masculine' topic to discuss, and that they open up and express themselves about a 'women's issue.' The following extract from his PhD thesis explains how both the participants and himself as a researcher (also a young man at university) approached this:

> In all of the focus groups there may have been some initial trepidation in this respect. There was typically a sense of discomfiture when the discussions began, and that participants were unsure of how to behave in this unfamiliar environment, discussing a potentially unfamiliar topic. It seemed as though they were looking to each other in an attempt to gauge what the appropriate way to behave in this context was, and what were appropriate things for young men to say about partner violence with their peer group. In my research diary, I wrote after the first focus group:
>
> > When I then started talking about my research, I could see that familiar look on their faces, of when you are trying to talk to men about something which men are not 'supposed' to talk about, that look of vulnerability and insecurity mixed with trying to preserve the outer shell of masculine 'toughness.' I was also worried at this point that maybe they would not be very cooperative with me – I confess that I still feel nervous about raising these kinds of issues with a group of men, because you just never know what kind of reaction you're going to get, and they could all just laugh at you.

However, this sense of unease usually dissipated relatively quickly, as one of the young men after another began to become engaged in the discussion, and it became clear that it was acceptable for them to do so in this homosocial setting. In order to try and facilitate this, I did everything I could to help them feel at ease in the discussion, by treating the discussion as informal, relaxed and friendly as possible, reassuring the participants and validating their responses whenever possible, and encouraging them to make whatever contributions they wished to in relation to the discussion – or none at all, if they preferred.

(Burrell, 2018, p. 110)

In the end, Burrell reflected that discussions flowed and a substantial amount of rich and in-depth data was produced, with the participants offering a wide range of nuanced responses.

Designing interview or focus group question guides

In outlining the example of Bows' work with older women, it was noted that older people might prefer a more conversational style within interviews. In fact, this is a style that works well generally when interviewing or running focus groups, as it puts the interviewee more at ease and allows them to feel that they have some control over the direction of the discussion. This is particularly important when interviewing survivors of violence and abuse (who typically have had control taken away from them as part of their experience of violence and abuse). One way to help participants feel a sense of control during the interview is to ensure that the start and the end of the interview are well designed and specified within the interview schedule.

Going in 'cold' when talking about experiences of violence and abuse can be difficult for participants, especially when they might otherwise have been thinking about other topics such as what to feed the children for tea, whether the grass was dry enough to mow, or how best to care for a sick relative. In light of this, it is useful for the researcher to begin an interview with an 'easy' opener. In some cases, the data from this question will not even be used in the analysis – the question's purpose is simply to help make the interviewee (and interviewer) feel more comfortable and to provide a context for the rest of the interview. In addition to the use of 'small talk,' asking what 'prompted' someone to participate in the research can also be a useful question to ask near the start of the interview (see Box 4.1).

Box 4.1

First two questions from Bows' interviews with older women

1   Can you tell me a little bit about yourself?
   ● Have you always lived in the area?
   ● Do you have any children/grandchildren?
   ● Do you have any hobbies?
2   Can you tell me a little bit about how why you have decided to talk to me today? (Prompt – why do you think taking part in this study is important?)

This approach is not only useful when interviewing survivors or perpetrators of violence and abuse, but can also be important when interviewing practitioners or policy makers. Whilst these interviewees may be less personally affected by the subject matter than victim-survivors, an 'easy' start to the interview can still be beneficial to the process. In the example in Box 4.2, the first question provides the function of showing that the interviewer is interested in the background of the practitioner themselves and the context/any professional backgrounds that might be relevant to the project. The second question acts as an 'easy' warm-up question given that it is about the practitioner's day to day work. It also allows the researcher to assess whether there are any inconsistencies in the way that different staff within the same organisation or across different agencies describe the intervention itself.

Box 4.2

First two questions evaluating a set of multi-agency interventions

1   Could you tell me a bit about your background and how you came to be working in this position for [support organisation]?
2   Could you talk us through the [support organisation] intervention you are part of?

A different approach to beginning a semi-structured interview is shown in Box 4.3. These were the first two questions asked in Project Mirabal to men attending community domestic violence perpetrator programmes and also to the women partners/ex-partners of men attending such programmes. In this example, the second question (1.2) looks at first sight to be a 'big' question to introduce so early in the interview process. The rest of the questions in this section were about gender roles and stereotypes within society, and how these gender roles and stereotypes played out within the interviewee's relationship. Whilst these questions might have been better 'warm up' questions than asking about the events that led to their or their partner/ex-partner's involvement in a domestic violence perpetrator programme, the researchers' previous experience was that participants often come prepared to tell 'their story,' and that it can sometimes be useful to give them the space to tell this early on, especially if the interviews are long, as in this example. This technique of allowing participants the space to provide any information they wanted to share near the beginning of the interview ensured that they wouldn't feel the need to 'shoe-horn' this information in later on. Within this specific project, participants varied considerably in the level of detail they provided in response to the question (Box 4.3; question 1.2), ranging from very long answers with a lot of detail about specific acts of violence (often identified as 'the worst it had got'), to very short answers such as 'we were having problems and my social worker suggested we come here.'

Box 4.3

First two questions from Project Mirabal

1.1 Can you tell me about your relationship with [name]? (Try to include the information below, if not collect in demographics section)

Relationship status: current/ex-partner
Relationship type: married/living together/separated/other
Length of relationship:
Number of children:

1.2 Can you tell me about the events that led up to your involvement with [name of the project]?

It can be useful to break up interview schedules into specific parts, or sections. This helps to group questions that are linked to the same research question or topic, supports the conversational/interview flow and can assist with timekeeping in cases where there are particular time limits placed on the interviews. Whilst this is useful advice for interviewing generally, in terms of interviewing violence and abuse survivors, it can also be used to provide interviewees with a sense of what is coming, the sort of questions they will be asked and where they are at in the interview as they go along. This can help participants feel more in control of the process. For example, Project Mirabal involved a long interview schedule, and it was helpful at the start of the interview to be able to tell the participant that there were three sets of questions in the interview, the first about themselves and their relationship, the second addressing specific examples of things that happened with their partner or ex-partner and the third about their experience of the project that they had been receiving support from (Box 4.4). Having these distinct sections meant that the interviewee could be clearer about where they were 'at' in the interview.

Box 4.4

Project Mirabal, example of phase structure in interview schedule

Section three: project questions

We are now at the third section and are nearly finished. In this part I'd like us to talk about your experience of the project. This set of questions therefore relate to present situations, since [name] has been on the DVPP and since you were contacted by the WSW.

It is also worth giving thought to how the interview will be ended. In Project Mirabal, these were the questions that were asked of the female partners and ex-partners of the men attending domestic violence perpetrator programmes (Box 4.5).

Box 4.5

Project Mirabal, example of final questions and debrief

Thank you this is all really useful. I am now going to ask you a couple of questions about the future.

3.2.8   Do you think [name] can or will change as a result of the Programme? (If no, what would make him change?)

3.2.9   What is the one thing he can do that would make the biggest difference to your life?

3.2.10   What else would make the biggest difference to your life?

Prompts: more support, money, employment, childcare

Debrief [after recording halted]

- How do you feel now we are at the end of the interview?
- Is there anything you would like to talk more about?
- Is there anything you would like to get more support with?
- Is there anything you would like to ask us?

In this example, ending the interview with questions about the future rather than about past experiences was designed as a way of moving the interviewee back into the present. Most often, this resulted in a positive ending to the interview, with participants thinking about the things that needed to change in their lives, either in terms of their partner and his behaviour or in terms of life more generally. However, this was not always the case, and in one interview the question about whether she thought her partner would change as a result of the programme led the participant to become upset and start crying, having experienced a sudden realisation that no, she did not believe he would make changes. However, this is an exception, and even though this person became upset, she later said that it had made her 'admit things to herself.' As a result, this end to the interview could still have had some positive effects for her even though her initial reaction was not as positive as might have been expected.

Managing 'big voices' within focus groups

Focus groups are less common than semi-structured interviews in violence and abuse research, and are often more used for opinions on a given topic. Smithson (2000) highlights the moderator strategies that are sometimes required when running focus groups, including when dealing with one or several dominant voices within a group that can result in only one opinion being 'heard.' She argues that it is crucial not only to look at better moderator techniques, but also to analyse focus groups in a way that takes account of these potential issues. In a research project on what 'justice' means for survivors of sexual violence, one of the authors (Westmarland) led two group discussions – one of with a group of people who had similar backgrounds and were of a similar age range, and one with people who had more diverse backgrounds and were drawn from a broader age range. The dynamics in each of the groups was very different, with the latter containing an example of where a small number of 'big' voices put forward such an extreme notion of 'justice' (for them, castration) that it made it difficult for more liberal views to be put forward. Box 4.6 contains an excerpt from the group where part of the conversation started off about sex offender treatment programmes, moved on to issues relating to chemical castration and then moved on to a discussion about surgical castration.

Box 4.6

Excerpt from group discussion on 'justice' and sexual violence

P4   If there was a punishment of castration, do you think that would put a lot of men off?

P2   Yeah.

F   Surgical rather than chemical castration?

[General laughter]

P2   Well if . . . like if a rapist was actually castrated they couldn't rape people by definition anymore.

P4   If you know you've got the right person just, is it cut the balls off, do you? But, you know, but you have to make sure that you've got absolutely the right person and that's where capital punishment kind of went out the window didn't it because we got the wrong people.

[Murmurs of agreement]

P4   So if it's absolutely bang on, that's it, then – chop?

F   So which sexual offences would we be doing actual full castration? If we felt we knew, you know, beyond reasonable doubt that it was that person?

P1   Anything to do with children.

P2   All of them, I think.

P1   Yeah, all of them, yeah.

F   All of them? Even indecent exposure?

[Murmurs of agreement]

P5   I'm not sure . . .

P4   Exposure, there are a lot of people who . . . you have to go into the psychology of why they do that because it doesn't actually mean that they're going to have sex with anyone.

[Murmurs of agreement]

[. . .]

P5   I don't agree with the . . . erm . . . where somebody's in a nightclub, and they've touched somebody, I don't agree they should be castrated.

P6   No, no, no, no, no.

In this case, there seemed to be some agreement with the idea of castration for certain categories of sexual offence, but the voices were limited to a small number of the participants. Challenges were made in relation to some of the offences that are generally considered to be less serious than rape, but at the time no one challenged the idea that rapists, especially men who raped children, should be surgically castrated. After the group discussion, individual

semi-structured interviews explored notions of 'justice' in relation to participants' individual experiences of sexual violence, as it was felt that this topic
would be better explored in a one-to-one conversation rather than in a group
discussion. In some of these interviews, it became clear that some of the participants had been interested in exploring issues such as restorative justice
but had felt unable to raise such 'liberal' views against such a strong, punitive
standpoint in the group.

Interviewing with 'insider/outsider' status

At first glance it appears relatively straightforward to position the role of the
researcher (an 'outsider') as separate and distinct from any support or practitioner ('insider') role that the participant may require. This distinction is typically
made clear through a process whereby the researcher will close the interview
and then go on to ensure that the participant's support needs are being met,
making additional referrals where required (see also Chapter 2). In some cases
though, this distinction between researcher and practitioner is less clear, and
roles can become entangled. Many practitioners are involved in research, either
as part of their job description, in partnership with academics, as part time PhD
researchers or as full time PhD researchers working as part of a partnership
arrangement, such as a Knowledge Transfer Partnership where project supervision is shared between the university and an organisation. Whilst this might
be seen by as complicated, with 'messy' boundaries which could create ethical
and other limitations, this would be to take a pessimistic view of what such projects can achieve. Rather, these projects can provide more in-depth information
about a topic. McRobbie (1991) stated that

> [a] researcher visiting a girl's project regularly and talking to the girls as a
> researcher, will come up with a different account of the girls and the project,
> than would the full-time worker.
>
> (McRobbie, 1991, p. 69)

This was the situation encountered by Maddy Coy, who undertook her PhD
research on the links between women's experiences of local authority care and
routes into selling sex, whilst at the same time working as an outreach worker
in a health promotion service for women. The research was incorporated into
her everyday work, for example she carried out research interviews and then
provided follow-up support. She also fed emerging findings back into the service to help shape provision. In this way Coy was both an 'insider' as a practitioner and an 'outsider' as a researcher.

Coy used life history interviews (where the interview focuses on the whole life course or specific issues that have affected different stages of the life course) combined with feminist ethnography (see Chapter 9) alongside her role as an outreach worker, and she provides a reflexive account of this dual role in her article 'This morning I'm a researcher, this afternoon I'm an outreach worker: Ethical dilemmas in practitioner research' (Coy, 2006). She explains that the use of life history interviews allowed the women participants to make their own connections between being in care and selling sex in a more holistic way than other methods might have allowed:

> When listening to the women's accounts, it was clear that the circumstances of their early lives had been well rehearsed through interviews with various professionals such as social workers and probation officers. Most of the women said they had never been asked about all of their lives, only the aspects relevant to each professional (offending behaviour, drug use, homelessness).
>
> (Coy, 2006, p. 423)

The interviews took place in a range of different locations, including the outreach project base and the women's homes, and varied in length between half an hour and three hours. The interviews and ethnography were part of a wider participatory action research (PAR) approach to the research questions, and Coy explained this approach to potential participants:

> When introducing the research I made it clear to the women that my experiences had led me to believe that the lives of young women in the care system who had entered prostitution had not been heard, that I did not possess the knowledge necessary to inform interventions, and as those who had lived it they were the agents of change who could make their stories heard anonymously and collectively through myself.
>
> (Coy, 2006, p. 426)

In some cases, Coy found that conducting life history interviews was beneficial to her role as a support worker – enabling her to understand more about the issues the women were facing and of how the women made sense of their lives. In other cases, it was because of her knowledge of some women's situations that meant she did not feel able to invite them to participate in her research, as shown in one of her research diary excerpts:

> Tanya was heavily pregnant, using both heroin and crack, being abused by her partner, and sleeping rough when I met her through street outreach.

Throughout our appointments with various service providers, she spoke little, only to ask me why I was helping her – as nobody had ever done anything
for her without expecting something in return. At one appointment she told
a health worker that she had been in care during her adolescence. Although
she was unaware of the research, I felt that it would be inappropriate to
discuss this with her in case she felt that this was the only reason I was supporting her. Building trust and rapport with Tanya was time intensive, and I
did not reach a point where I felt my professional relationship with her was
established enough to ask if she would like to be involved in the research.

(Coy, 2006, pp. 421–422)

Coy argues that working as both practitioner and researcher represents a positive methodological approach, as it allows for the inclusion of follow-up support
to address any issues that are raised during the research process. However,
she notes that this method requires a reflexive approach which accommodates
potential power differentials between the researcher-practitioner and the participant. As in the case of Tanya, above, the research process was at times hindered by Coy's role as a practitioner first and foremost, something that would
not have been the case had the researcher been external to the support pro-
cess/organisation. In spite of this, Coy concludes that overall the research ben-
efited from a deeper understanding of the women's lives, providing 'a privileged
access to their ontology' (Coy, 2006, p. 429).

Coy's (2006) work addresses the insider/outsider status from the position
of a practitioner-researcher. Another form of insider/outsider approach was
taken by Burrell (2018) as part of his PhD research. Burrell (2018) interviewed
pro-feminist activist men about their work with men and boys to end violence
against women. Positioning himself both as activist (insider) and researcher
(outsider), he describes himself as taking a 'critical friend' position (Costa and
Kallick, 1993), following Flood's (2015) approach of 'cheerleading' such work
with men and boys but also being critical about its potential drawbacks. Burrell
(2018) states,

This is not always an easy position to adopt – especially when having a
face to face discussion with individuals who are involved in actually doing
that work. For example, at times I questioned the extent to which I had the
right to critique the work that interviewees were doing on the ground, as a
researcher looking on, rather than being an active contributor. On occasion,
I felt a small degree of confusion or even scepticism between myself and
the interviewees about my role in relation to their work – was I really part
of this movement of activists, or more of an observer, watching on from
the side-lines? At times, I questioned whether being a researcher inevitably

places one in an 'outsider' position to some extent in relation to what is being researched – and whether this is a bad thing or not.

(Burrell, 2018, p. 89)

Whilst acting with both insider and outsider status can therefore be difficult, Coy and Burrell have demonstrated that this status can be managed with a reflexive approach. The insider/outsider status should be linked into the analysis, and 'held on to' as key context to the overall findings and recommendations.

Impacts on participants

Most of the issues relating to participant distress overlap with ethical considerations, which are discussed in detail in Chapter 3. However, it is useful to briefly reflect on participant distress within this chapter as well, given that the first point of the World Health Organisation's (WHO) ethical considerations for conducting research is that 'the safety of respondents and the research team is paramount and should infuse all project decisions' (Watts et al., 2001, p. 2).

Many factors can affect the way participants respond to being interviewed. These include the questions that they are asked, the forms of violence and abuse that are addressed, how recently they experienced violence and abuse (or indeed if it is ongoing), how many times they have previously talked about their experiences and the amount of support they have received. Even the way a person is feeling on any given day is relevant; whether other things have gone wrong that day, whether they have felt rushed, whether they are tired – are all likely to have an impact. It should not be assumed that participants will become distressed whilst being interviewed, but likewise it should not be assumed that they will not – regardless of how long ago the violence and abuse happened. Bergen (1993), for example, found that a wide range of emotions were displayed within her research interviews on marital rape: '*Some were relatively unemotional and described the events much as if they were an outsider who had observed someone else being assaulted. Others became visibly distressed when remembering their past experiences.*' (Bergen, 1993, p. 208). However, she noted that even those who had become upset and experienced negative emotions such as flashbacks still described their experience of being a research participant as cathartic in some ways.

It is standard practice to remind participants at the start and during the interview that it is fine for them to stop the interview at any point and either return or not to return to it. Testa et al. (2011) state that, from their experience of interviewing sexual violence victim-survivors, it is rare for a survivor to stop an interview, even when the experience is upsetting to discuss. This is also the experience of the authors when interviewing participants about sexual violence and other forms of violence against women.

It is important that interviewers do not take a 'smash and grab' approach (Liamputtong, 2007), that is, getting in, doing the interview and leaving without any real interest in the participants. One example of how interviewers can avoid this approach and make their interviews more comfortable for participants is demonstrated by Baird and Mitchell's (2013) study of 11 women who had experienced domestic abuse during pregnancy. Following the WHO guidelines which were alluded to earlier, the authors reflected on their research study and shared some of the good practice that was utilised. Some of the points that can be taken from their reflection are:

- Building respectful relationships with (in their case) refuges is of crucial importance. Respectful relationships involve acknowledging not only that these organisations are busy and under multiple pressures, but also that they are placing the researcher in a privileged position by allowing them access to the refuge and to staff time,
- Relationships of reciprocity and trust should be maintained throughout the research, not as a one-off event,
- Play workers should be arranged for children wherever possible, to allow women to participate without being overheard by their children,
- Open questions can be used to develop a rapport with the participant (e.g. 'tell me a little about yourself'),
- If possible, researchers should meet participants before conducting the interview in order to verbally explain the research in more depth,
- Researchers should consider spending extra time at the refuge, taking biscuits and fruit to share, as a way of saying thank you to staff and participants,
- Researchers should avoid using terminology such as rape, violence or abuse, and instead should ask about specific acts such as being hit, slapped or beaten during their pregnancy (following Watts et al.'s (2001) recommendations),
- Researchers should recognise that any negative impact of the interview on the participant may not occur until after the interview finishes. Even when participants appear to be fine during the interview itself it can be useful for the researcher to follow-up with the participants, whether that be directly or via a support worker.

Baird and Mitchell (2013) found that interviewees typically managed their distress in the manner that was most comfortable for them as individuals. Some interviewees asked to pause the interviews when they became upset, returning to the interview after a break in which they had a cigarette or a drink, whilst other interviewees became upset but insisted that they wanted to continue with the interview without a break. The authors concluded that despite the distress that accompanied some of the interviews, many of the interviewees still expressed gratitude that their own views and feelings had been heard, acknowledged and fed into knowledge and practice.

Impact on researchers

It is not just research participants who may feel distress during or after participation in a research interview or focus group; researchers may also encounter difficult emotions, and possible impacts on researchers must also be considered. The impact of being a researcher who studies rape is considered in depth by Campbell (2002), in her book 'Emotionally Involved.' She connects her research, which involves thinking about rape for prolonged periods of time, interviewing rape survivors, and writing about rape, with her community volunteering as a rape victim advocate, which involves spending time in hospital emergency rooms, courtrooms and police departments. She highlights the need to make space for emotions and the analysis of such emotions as part of the research process: 'The difference between thinking and feeling does not have to be so painstakingly created, maintained, and reinforced' (Campbell, 2002, p. 24). Hence, rather than seeing researcher emotions as problematic and something to be avoided or managed, from this perspective they can be a necessary and even useful part of the research process. Violence against women research, Campbell argues, represents a context where the interconnections between emotionality and science can be usefully interrogated.

Coles et al. (2014) analysed responses from an online message board alongside a small number of interviews to examine the trauma experienced by sexual violence researchers, investigating the main causes of distress for these researchers and what protective strategies they employed to cope with the distress. In terms of the trauma they experienced, the most common responses described by participants were 'anger, guilt and shame, fear, crying, and feeling sad and depressed' (Coles et al., 2014, p. 101). Some described issues such as nightmares and difficulties concentrating, which Coles et al. identified as suggestive of secondary traumatic stress, a clinical condition with symptoms similar to post traumatic stress disorder. Others appeared to be experiencing vicarious trauma, a phenomenon whereby an individual's worldview and inner experience is altered by their engagement with victim-survivors of trauma. The following examples illustrate the impact that working with trauma can have upon researchers.

After interviewing a woman who had been repeatedly raped and tortured as a young girl, I found myself feeling like I would vomit. Interestingly, I found that my reaction after the interview was worse than it was during the interview. I think that during the interview, I was so busy listening and responding that my reaction was delayed. I was also conscious of not wanting her to see how deeply her story had impacted on me and making sure that my distress didn't stop her speaking of her experience.

(SVRI discussion board, Female Researcher 1, Asia and South Pacific, in Coles et al., 2014, p. 101)

I remember well the initial physical sensation I experienced. It was deep bone-chilling coldness, which came whenever the women told me about the depths of their horror, terror, and torture. . . . Whenever I am writing from that emotional place of horror, I still experience deep-seated coldness, and my ears feel congested, and I feel flu-like. This lasts for the length of time that I am immersed in such [emotionally] deep writing.

(SVRI discussion board 2009, Female Researcher 1, North America, in Coles et al., 2014, p. 101)

One of the main causes of distress for researchers was knowing that there was a systematic neglect of victims; their research participants needed services that were not available to them. For example, one participant talked of knowing that he needed to act, but not knowing what to do or where to refer.

In terms of coping strategies, Coles et al. (2014) recommend the following approach based on their findings:

- *Preparation:* it is important that researchers carry information on related issues such as how sexual assault is defined, the wide range of responses to sexual assault and the services available to people who have experienced sexual assault. This is particularly necessary in resource-poor settings.
- *Debriefing, support and supervision:* researchers should have access to formal and informal support systems, including formal counselling and psychotherapy if needed. They should be provided with supportive, scheduled supervision with managers and supervisors.
- *Self-care:* in addition to more structured support, researchers should be encouraged to practice self-care. As might be expected, self-care strategies utilised by the participants in Coles et al.'s study were varied and individual. They included creative pursuits such as painting and cooking; physical activities such as gardening and having massages; communal activities such as spending time with family, friends and communities; and/or spiritual activities involving the practice of their faith.

Coles et al. (2014) conclude that peers and colleagues are an important source of support to researchers, but that external resources should also be made available outside the supervisory relationship. In addition, research teams should be supportive and provide safe emancipatory spaces for discussions about challenging issues and physical and psychological well-being.

Impact on transcribers and administrators

There is a dearth of literature on aspects of the transcribing process that need to be considered in relation to violence and abuse interviews or focus groups. Generally speaking, there is little discussion in relation to the impact of transcribing certain topics on either the researcher-transcriber or on professional transcribers – the latter being increasingly common within social research. Where researcher-transcribers are doing the transcriptions themselves, the transcription process has traditionally been seen as a positive and important part of the analysis process – part of immersion in the analytical process and delving 'deeper' into the data. When that data is traumatic to read, because it is upsetting in nature per se and/or because it triggers previous experiences of trauma for the transcriber themselves, this immersive experience can be challenging.

Etherington (2007) is one of the few to consider the experiences of a transcriber working with traumatic stories – in her case the lives of people who had experienced traumatic childhood experiences and subsequently misused drugs. As a therapist who also works in research, Etherington is required by her professional UK body the British Association for Counselling and Psychotherapy (BACP) to undergo regular external supervision of at least an hour and a half. This is required for various reasons, including to protect psychotherapists and counsellors from 'burnout.' Despite knowing that experiencing vicarious trauma was possible and taking steps to prevent it during her therapeutic work, Etherington was nevertheless unprepared for it when it occurred in relation to a previous research study with which she was involved. This led her to be more aware of the potential needs of her administrator when she asked for additional work transcribing interviews in Etherington's (2007) traumatic childhood and drugs project:

> Since then [experiencing vicarious trauma] I resolved that I would never again expose myself – or others involved with me in this kind of work – to that kind of experience. . . . I became aware that I also needed to consider my duty of care towards her [the administrator doing the transcribing] as someone without clinical training, experience or supervision, who was listening to traumatic stories closely and over and over again.
>
> (Etherington, 2007, p. 87)

For the transcriber in this situation, it was being aware of the general content of the interview in advance and also having an opportunity to debrief that she found most helpful. However, Etherington (2007) acknowledges that in some instances no personal relationship exists between researchers and transcribers. Given the increase in globalised transcription services over the last decade, the absence of this relationship is even more likely now than it was ten years ago when Etherington was writing.

Conducting feminist interviews with men

Interviewing men, either as perpetrators, victim-survivors or other stakeholders, can bring with it different dynamics when conducting feminist research interviews or focus groups. Interviewing violent men is a topic that has generated much discussion between violence and abuse researchers, with many who have undertaken such a task reflecting on the challenges and dilemmas that come with it. Just as there is no single experience of interviewing a victim of violence and abuse, there are many different experiences of interviewing violent men. Cavanagh and Lewis (1996) conducted interviews with violent men as part of a longitudinal evaluation of programmes for perpetrators of domestic abuse. They note,

> We spent over 300 hours listening to men excuse, deny, minimize and blame. Some have cried, some have raged, some have laughed, some have flirted, some have challenged. Some have sought to humour us, to enlist our sympathy, to control us, to outsmart us, to convince us.
>
> (Cavanagh and Lewis, 1996, p. 87)

There is no reason to assume that interviewing men who have used violence and abuse within a relationship will pose a physical risk to interviewers. Most men who use violence and abuse within relationships do not use violence against other people outside of the relationship (Hester et al., 2006). Rather it can be quite the opposite – in many cases coming across as a calm, peaceful, rational, likeable person is part of the power that abusive men hold over their victims. In Project Mirabal, some of the researchers commented that one of the most troubling things for them was just how likeable and 'normal' some of the men were.

This is not always the case though, and Cavanagh and Lewis (1996) found that some of the men in their study said things that they considered grossly offensive, for example describing women as 'sly devious bitches' or suggesting that violence is inevitably linked to masculinity. In some cases the researchers left interviews with unresolved difficulties about not being able to challenge men further due to their role as interviewers:

> We learned early on that many of the men we interviewed enjoyed nothing better than 'a good argument' during which they could demonstrate their (superior) knowledge and understanding of various issues. We sometimes had to disengage from such discussion, leaving the men thinking that he had 'won,' his attitudes reinforced. Similarly, when we felt less able to challenge, some men may have interpreted this as our empathising with their explanations, justifications or excuses. We left these interviews disappointed, confused, frustrated.
>
> (Cavanagh and Lewis, 1996, p. 108)

This experience echoes Smart's (1984) experience in her study on law, family and marriage, where she argues that a female feminist interviewer may experience research interviews with men as doubly oppressive, as she is not able to express alternative views, and placidly listening to sexist views reinforces the traditional male-female verbal exchange.

In Burrell's (2018) focus group interviews, the young men were not participating as victim-survivors or as perpetrators (although some of them may have fallen into one or both of these categories), but as a group of men who represent a demographic that is often targeted by prevention campaigns. Burrell (2018) reflected on the role that he had to play in terms of displaying a 'relatively "neutral" performance of masculinity' (Burrell, 2018, p. 116). He gave consideration to how much he, as a researcher, would challenge any overtly sexist or misogynist comments that might be displayed within the group. Because he worked with focus groups of up to nine men, he had responsibility for what others in the group might hear, adding additional complexities to what might exist in a one-to-one interview. Burrell sought to balance remaining silent (which he considered unethical) and intervening where necessary, for example if a discussion seemed focused on misunderstandings about violence and abuse. One of the ways he managed this balance was intervening through follow-up questions, attempting to provoke reflections, allowing other (less dominant) voices to be heard and keeping the group focused. Ultimately though, unless the discussion became offensive or based on inaccurate information, Burrell was clear that he appreciated hearing their views, regardless of whether he agreed with them or not:

> The principles commonly found within feminist research of attempting to minimise the power differentials between researcher and participants, and enabling participants to have their voices heard (even if I disagreed with them),

were held to be important even if the sample was made up of relatively privileged young men. This was both as a political commitment, and also to enable the production of more insightful data, in the expectation that the young men would be more likely to be honest and candid if they felt able to speak openly without being judged or under any pressure from the researcher.

(Burrell, 2018, p. 113)

Lee (1997) also reflected on her experiences of interviewing men – in her case from the perspective of a young, white, able bodied, heterosexual woman interviewing men about workplace sexual harassment. Because the interviews all addressed the topic of sexual harassment (although not all interviewees were necessarily perpetrators), Lee found herself increasingly reticent to interview men in private spaces. For nine of her interviews though, she reluctantly agreed to do so. In the run up to the interviews, she reflects on her concerns about the risks of doing this – particularly where she had agreed to interview men in their own homes. Some of the safety mechanisms she put in place in advance were: dressing plainly and 'primly,' with no jewellery or makeup – 'my clothing told them I had made no effort at all on their account' (Lee, 1997, p. 559) – and carrying a personal alarm. Although she doubted both of these strategies in terms of their potential effectiveness, she did reflect that at least if she was raped or murdered she was less likely to have been seen as partially responsible. In the end, the two experiences in which Lee felt most uncomfortable turned out to be during interviews in public places, for example in one case where the interviewee went to shake her hand at the end of the interview but just held her hand tightly while talking and not letting go instead of shaking it for a normal amount of time. Through these reflections, Lee expanded her notion of risky settings, and also emphasised the links between the method and the findings.

> Instead of concluding that my aversion to interviewing in private was, therefore misplaced, I would argue that risk can instead be seen as potentially present in public as well as in private. I would add that these incidents also usefully show how substantive data and methodology are inextricably linked.
>
> (Lee, 1997, p. 562)

Summary

This chapter has described some of the issues that can arise when interviewing or conducting focus groups on gender, violence and abuse. It has drawn on particular examples of where these methods have been put into practice, offered practical tips that have worked well in the authors' own research and shown how reflection on the research process itself is a central concern which should be considered a core part of the analytical process.

References

Baird, K. and Mitchell, T. (2013) Issues for consideration by researchers conducting sensitive research with women who have endured domestic violence during pregnancy, *Evidence Based Midwifery*, *11*(1), pp. 21–27.

Bergen, R. K. (1993) Interviewing survivors of marital rape: Doing feminist research on sensitive topics, In: C. M. Renzetti and R. M. Lee (Eds.) *Researching Sensitive Topics* (pp. 197–211). Newbury Park, CA: Sage.

Burrell, S. (2018) *Engaging Men and Boys in the Prevention of Men's Violence Against Women in the UK*. Doctoral Thesis, Durham: Durham University.

Campbell, R. (2002) *Emotionally Involved: The Impact of Researching Rape*. New York, NY: Routledge.

Cavanagh, K. and Lewis, R. (1996) Interviewing violent men: Challenge or compromise?, In: K. Cavanagh and V. Cree (Eds.) *Working with Men: Feminism and Social Work* (pp. 87–112). London: Psychology Press.

Chantler, K., Gangoli, G. and Hester, M. (2009) Forced marriage in the UK: Religious, cultural, economic or state violence?, *Critical Social Policy*, *29*(4), pp. 587–612.

Coles, J., Astbury, J., Dartnall, E. and Limjerwala, S. (2014) A qualitative exploration of researcher trauma and researchers' responses to investigating sexual violence, *Violence against Women*, *20*(1), pp. 95–117.

Corbin, J. and Morse, J. M. (2003) The unstructured interactive interview: Issues of reciprocity and risks when dealing with sensitive topics, *Qualitative Inquiry*, *9*(3), pp. 335–354.

Costa, A. and Kallick, B. (1993) Through the lens of a critical friend, *Educational Leadership*, *51*(2), pp. 49–51.

Coy, M. (2006) This morning I'm a researcher, this afternoon I'm an outreach worker: Ethical dilemmas in practitioner research, *International Journal of Social Research Methodology*, *9*(5), pp. 419–431.

Etherington, K. (2007) Working with traumatic stories: From transcriber to witness, *International Journal of Social Research Methodology*, *10*(2), pp. 85–97.

Flood, M. (2015) Work with men to end violence against women: A critical stocktake, *Culture, Health and Sexuality*, *17*(2), pp. 159–176.

Fontana, A. and Frey, J. H. (1994) Interviewing: The art of science, In: N. Denzin and Y. Lincoln (Eds.) *The Handbook of Qualitative Research* (pp. 361–376). Thousand Oaks, CA: Sage.

Gangoli, G., Gill, A., Mulvihill, N. and Hester, M. (2018) Perception and barriers: Reporting female genital mutilation, *Journal of Aggression, Conflict and Peace Research*, Epub ahead of print 7 January 2018. DOI: 10.1108/JACPR-09-2017-0323.

Gill, A. K., Begikhani, N. and Hague, G. (2012) 'Honour'-based violence in Kurdish communities, *Women's Studies International Forum*, *35*(2), pp. 75–85.

Hague, G., Thiara, R. and Mullender, A. (2011) Disabled women, domestic violence and social care: The risk of isolation, vulnerability and neglect, *British Journal of Social Work*, *41*(1), pp. 148–165.

Hester, M., Westmarland, N., Gangoli, G., Wilkinson, M., O'Kelly, C., Kent, A. and Diamond, A. (2006) *Domestic Violence Perpetrators: Identifying Needs to Inform Early Intervention*. Bristol: University of Bristol, Northern Rock Foundation and Home Office.

Khoshnami, M. S., Mohammadi, E., Rasi, H. A., Khankeh, H. R. and Arshi, M. (2017) Conceptual model of acid attacks based on survivor's experiences: Lessons from a qualitative exploration, *Burns*, *43*(3), pp. 608–618.

Lee, D. (1997) Interviewing men: Vulnerabilities and dilemmas, *Women's Studies International Forum*, 20(4), pp. 553–564.

Liamputtong, P. (2007) *Researching the Vulnerable*. London: Sage.

McRobbie, A. (1991) *Feminism and Youth Culture: From Jackie to Just Seventeen*. Basingstoke: Palgrave Macmillan.

Minocha, S., Hartnett, E., Dunn, K., Evans, S., Heap, T., Middup, C. P., Murphy, B. and Roberts, D. (2013) *Conducting Empirical Research with Older People*, Designing for-and with-Vulnerable People, CHI 2013 Workshop, Paris, 27 April.

Morse, J. M. (2002) Interviewing the ill, In: J. F. Gubrium and J. A. Holstein, J. A. (Eds.) *Handbook of Interview Research: Context and Method* (pp. 317–328). London: Sage.

Reinharz, S. and Davidman, L. (1992) *Feminist Methods in Social Research*. Oxford: Oxford University Press.

Rubin, H. J. and Rubin, I. S. (1995) *Qualitative Interviewing: The Art of Hearing Data*. Thousand Oaks, CA: Sage.

Smart, C. (1984) *The Ties That Bind: Law, Marriage and the Reproduction of Patriarchal Relations*. London: Routledge & Kegan Paul.

Smithson, J. (2000) Using and analyzing focus groups: Limitations and possibilities, *International Journal of Social Research Methodology*, 3(2), pp. 103–119.

Testa, M., Livingston, J. A. and VanZile-Tamsen, C. (2011) Advancing the study of violence against women using mixed methods: Integrating qualitative methods into a quantitative research programme, *Violence against Women*, 17(11), pp. 236–250.

Watts, C., Heise, L., Ellsberg, L. H. and Ellsberg, M. (2001) *Putting Women First: Ethical and Safety Recommendations for Research on Domestic Violence against Women*. Geneva: World Health Organization.

6 Conducting surveys

Although research on gender violence is often associated with qualitative methods, quantitative surveys have long been used in feminist research. Indeed, surveys represent one of the primary methods used to gather data on the prevalence of different forms of violence against women. As such, survey data makes a fundamental contribution to both theories and concepts of gender and violence (Walby and Towers, 2016). To this end, the present chapter will examine the utility of surveys in violence against women research and consider some of the specific considerations researchers face when using this method.

Background

The opening chapter of this book considered what made research 'feminist' and whether a 'feminist methodology' could be identified. It was concluded that no single feminist methodology exists, and no specific method that can be viewed as inherently feminist. Rather, a feminist approach is concerned with the underlying principles that influence the way research is conducted. That said, one of the strongest criticisms of 'malestream' social research has been that it relies too heavily on quantitative methods, particularly surveys. These quantitative methods, it is argued, have excluded women and failed to capture the lived experience of violence against women (Tolman and Szalacha, 1999; Sarantakos, 2012).

However, it is not the survey as a method that is of concern here, but how it is used. Indeed, surveys have a long and rich history in gender, violence and abuse research and continue to be an important method for understanding the extent, nature and trends in violence against women globally. For example, the creation of the Sexual Experiences Survey in 1987 (Koss et al., 1987) pioneered a new approach to the collection of data on the prevalence of sexual victimisation. Over the previous four decades, data on violence against women has been collected using population surveys (Myhill, 2017), as well as with dedicated surveys which examine violence against women specifically or include it as a module in a larger victimisation survey. Much of this research has focused on estimates of the prevalence of domestic violence, though feminists have raised concerns about the ability of these data to capture an accurate picture of gendered violence and coercive control within relationships (Hagemann-White, 2001).

Gender, violence and abuse researchers in England and Wales have been mainly reliant on special modules being added to the Crime Survey England and Wales, previously the British Crime Survey (BCS). Although steps have been taken over the years to improve the quality of data within this survey, there have historically been many problems with the way the survey measures violence against women. Taking sexual violence as an example, very few women reported rape to the BCS; in the 1983 sweep only one woman disclosed an attempted rape in the whole of the survey sample (Hough and Mayhew, 1983). This led to a period of time when the results for rape were simply not included in the BCS publications because so few disclosures were made (Percy and Mayhew, 1997). However, disclosure rates increased in the mid-1990s when the Computer Assisted Self-Interviewing (CASI) method was introduced (for more discussion of this approach see Mirrlees-Black, 1999; Walby and Allen, 2004).

Walby et al. (2016) suggest there are three main reasons for using surveys to collect data on violent crime (as opposed to using police recorded crime statistics). First, violent crimes are underreported to the police. Second, the violent crimes that are reported to the police are not representative of the true pattern of violence (for example, violence committed by someone known to the victim is less likely to be reported than violence committed by a stranger). Third, the quality of the data within police recorded crime statistics has been called into question. As Walby and Towers (2017, p. 12) state, 'A survey is one of the best ways to discover the extent and distribution of violence, including comparisons over time and between locations.'

This is particularly true for violence for against women, which is chronically underreported; it is estimated that 85 percent of sexual offences go unreported to the police (Ministry of Justice, 2013). Moreover, there are serious problems with the way police (do not) record gender violence offences leading to many cases being no-crimed or no-further actioned; a recent report by Her Majesty's Inspectorate of Constabulary (HMIC) concluded that 1 in 4 sexual offences should have been recorded as crimes but were not (HMIC, 2014). The reasons cited for this were mainly centred around poor processes for recording the crimes and for transferring them on to national recording systems.

Designing surveys

Surveys in gender violence and abuse research are generally used to capture data on the prevalence/extent of violence, trends in the incidence of violence, the nature of the violence and the characteristics of the victims and perpetrators. There are a number of specific considerations which should be taken into account when designing surveys for use in violence and abuse research.

Survey design - standalone or incorporated approaches

There are two broad approaches to violence against women survey research: surveys on broader issues/crime which incorporate questions on violence against women, and standalone surveys which capture data specifically on violence against women. Both approaches have strengths and limitations.

General surveys which include questions about violence against women

The first type of survey, which incorporates gender, violence and abuse questions within a broader scope of research, is commonly used across the West and has provided a long-standing source of data on violence against women. These surveys are typically population-based victimisation surveys which include one or more sections dedicated to violence and abuse. Examples of these surveys include the National Victimisation Survey (USA), the General Social Survey (Canada) and the Crime Victimisation Survey (Australia). In England and Wales, the annual Crime Survey for England and Wales (CSEW; formerly named the British Crime Survey) captures data on a range of criminal offences and includes a 'module' which asks about experiences of interpersonal crime. This survey has several benefits; it can capture large sample sizes which allow for extrapolation of the data to generate prevalence estimates, and the frequency of data collection facilitates observation of trends in these offences.

A key strength of the CSEW is the range of victimisation it captures. The survey first incorporated a dedicated domestic violence module in 1996, when a computerised self-completion module was added to the survey. This questionnaire covered physical assaults and frightening threats committed by either current or former partners (Mirrlees-Black, 1999). In 1998 stalking and sexual victimisation were also included. In 2001, all three forms of violence were included in an expanded 'interpersonal violence' self-completion module which incorporated domestic violence, sexual assault and stalking against both men and women. This allowed for the examination of distinct forms of sexual assault

(Walby and Allen, 2004). Since 2001 the CSEW has continued to collect data on these offences, measuring participants' experiences over the previous year as well as their experiences since the age of 16.

The CSEW's inclusion of domestic violence, sexual assault and stalking in the same module allows for analysis of the relationships between these forms of violence. However, unlike the original 2001 version of the self-completion survey (Walby and Allen, 2004), recent versions measure the frequency of intimate partner violence across all abusive acts of different kinds, making it impossible to separate out specific types of violence. Moreover, the survey only captures violent crime committed by an intimate partner; it does not capture violent crime committed by strangers, acquaintances, friends or other family members. Consequently, the self-completion module does not provide data from which estimates of the number of violent crimes can be made (Walby et al., 2016).

A further problem is that victims may not define their experiences as falling within the remit of a 'crime' survey (Mirrlees-Black, 1999) For example, in older versions of the National Victimisation Survey in the USA, the questions asked were fairly broad and did not specifically focus on experiences that were perpetrated by a partner/someone known to the victim. Given that violence within intimate relationships has historically been considered somewhat normative (e.g. marital rape was legal in some US states until 1993), it is likely that many participants will not have considered their relationship when answering questions about violence and victimisation. In 1994 the survey was redesigned to include a specific question asking whether various types of behaviour had ever been perpetrated by someone at work/school, neighbours, friends, relatives or other family members. This led to an increase in the overall prevalence estimate for domestic violence against women, with figures rising from 0.3 percent prior to the redesign to 0.9 percent after the redesign (Mirrlees-Black, 1999).

Standalone surveys measuring violence against women

The second style of survey, standalone surveys which specifically address one or more forms of violence against women, are also widely used. These have been conducted on an (inter)national scale, as in the case of the European Union survey on violence against women but are also commonly used in academic, think tank and public/third sector research. Examples include:

- Equality and Human Rights Commission (2018) survey on sexual harassment in the workplace
- YouGov (2012) survey on sexual harassment on public transport
- National Union of Students (2018) survey on sexual violence universities.

Standalone surveys tend to yield higher prevalence rates than general surveys which include some questions on violence against women. This may be because of the way violence against women is defined and measured by the two types of survey, or because standalone surveys may be more likely to show bias in the sample selection. For example, standalone surveys on violence against women are more likely to be used by researchers with an interest in the field whose access to participants (relative to non-specialist researchers) will be more skewed towards those who have experienced violence.

Example 1: European Union Agency for Fundamental Rights (FRA) violence against women: an EU-wide survey (2014)

This large-scale survey was conducted across 28 Member States of the European Union (EU). It was based on interviews with 42,000 women across the EU. Within each Member State the survey covered all women aged 18 to 74 years who were living in the Member State in question and who spoke at least one of the official languages of the country.

The FRA survey asked about women's experiences of violence by describing various acts of violence (behaviour questions) in as concrete terms as possible. Two approaches were adopted to capture data: face-to-face interviews and a short self-completion questionnaire. The aim of the self-completion questionnaire was to offer women the opportunity to disclose their experiences of violence in a more anonymous manner. Respondents were asked to complete the short paper questionnaire on their own, without the assistance of the interviewer, and to seal it in an envelope which would not be opened by the interviewer and which was delivered separately to the central research team.

The requirements for interviewers on this project were different from those typically required by research companies. All interviewers selected to work had to be female and have a minimum of three months' experience of random probability survey work.

Defining violence against women within surveys

One of the most important considerations in designing any survey, regardless of the methodological approach, is the use of terminology and the need to ensure that all participants will understand the questions being asked. However, there are additional factors to consider in violence against women research around the terms used and how these terms are defined and understood. For example, in the UK it is common to see violence that is perpetrated by a partner or spouse defined as 'domestic violence.' However, this terminology is rarely used in other jurisdictions; for example, the US tend to use narrow terms such as 'intimate-partner violence,' or broader terms such as 'familial violence.' A further issue is one of differential interpretation; one person's understanding of the terms 'violence' or 'abuse' can vary substantially from another person's interpretation of these terms.

Moreover, even within these broader umbrella definitions (domestic violence/familial violence) the range of behaviours captured by specific terms can vary. For example, 'sexual violence' is included in most definitions of domestic violence/familial violence and intimate partner violence, but this term itself lacks unification. For example, Germany conducted a national violence against women study in 2003, the first of its kind in the country (Müller et al., 2003). The study utilised a sample of 10,264 women aged 18 to 85 years and involved face-to-face interviews supplemented with questionnaires. The central forms of violence examined by the study were physical violence, sexual violence, sexual harassment and psychological abuse. The study focused on longitudinal experience, asking women about their experiences of each form of abuse since the age of 16. The items on sexual violence were based on a narrow definition of violence, exclusively focusing on explicitly criminal forms of sexual violence such as rape, attempted rape and various forms of sexual coercion involving the use of physical force or threat. This definition therefore excluded sexual harassment and other forms of sexual violence, such as indecent exposure and revenge pornography.

More recently, Nguyen et al. (2018) reported on the results of the Violence against Children Survey conducted in Malawi and Nigeria. The survey sampled female and male individuals aged 13 to 24, and included questions designed to measure experiences of childhood sexual, physical and emotional violence. The survey defined sexual violence as

> (a) unwanted sexual touching (e.g., touching in a sexual way, kissing, grabbing, or fondling), (b) attempted unwanted sexual intercourse (perpetrator attempted intercourse but penetration did not occur), (c) pressured intercourse (unwanted sex was completed through use of threats or nonphysical pressure), and (d) physically forced sex (unwanted intercourse completed through physical force).
>
> (Nguyen et al., 2018, p. 4)

This definition of sexual violence is limited to actual, or attempted, physical sexual violence through physical force or psychological pressure. It does not capture sexual harassment (such as unwanted comments of a sexual nature), sharing of intimate photos (or threats to do so) or other image-based sexual abuse behaviours such as up-skirting (see McGlynn and Rackley, 2018), nor does it include voyeurism or indecent exposure. Consequently, the range of sexually violent behaviours is limited in this survey.

In addition to the issues surrounding the adequate definition of core topics such as 'sexual violence,' surveys can also encounter problems in terms of the language that is used in the questions. The Sexual Experiences Survey has recently been revised following criticism of the survey design. This included concerns about the terminology, for example, the use of the term 'intercourse' which is now considered to be outdated and lacking in universal meaning (Johnson et al., 2017). Similarly, Johnson et al. (2017) note that other criticisms of the language related to the way that non-consent was operationalised; the phrase used in the original survey was 'when you didn't want to' which may not necessarily imply non-consent.

Question design and measurement

Surveys which seek to measure violence against women should give close consideration to the ways in which questions are asked and what the surveys actually measure. For example, the way in which respondents are asked if they have been raped is important. Participants may be more likely to disclose that they have been raped if they are asked 'have you ever been forced to have sex,' or 'have you ever been coerced into sex,' than if they are asked 'have you been raped?' despite the questions being essentially equivalent in their meaning (Lees, 1996).

It has been argued that questions that ask about specific types of behaviour in detail are better able to capture the prevalence of violence against women. One of the most widely used survey instruments is the Sexual Experiences Survey first designed and used by Koss et al. (1987). The innovation in this survey included behavioural descriptions of violent acts.

As Fisher (2009, p. 141) explains,

> A behaviorally specific question is one that does not ask simply if a respondent 'had been raped,' but rather describes an incident in graphic language that covers the elements of a criminal offense.

In a comparison of different survey question approaches, Fisher reports that the use of behaviour-specific questions 'appears to cue more women to recall what they had experienced' (Fisher, 2009, p. 143).

Example 2: Sexual Experiences Survey (Koss et al., 1987)

The Sexual Experiences Survey was designed and distributed by Koss and colleagues in 1987. The aim of the survey was to provide a more accurate picture of the extent of sexual victimisation, particularly 'hidden' rape (this is, rape that was not recorded by the police or captured in medical files). This was particularly important given that these recorded figures (which vastly underestimate the prevalence of sexual violence) were the two most common methods used to analyse the extent of sexual violence at the time.

The survey consisted of 13 closed (yes or no) questions which referred to sexual intercourse and various degrees of coercion, threat and force. The overarching question was 'have you ever' and the sub questions ranged from 'had sexual intercourse with a man/woman when you both wanted to?' to 'been in a situation where a man obtained sexual acts with you, such as anal or oral intercourse when you didn't want to by using threats or physical force?'

The survey was widely viewed as innovative in its methodology, not only in the style of questions (asking about specific behaviours) but also because the survey was designed to capture victimisation and perpetration. The same survey was handed to women (with victim focused questions) and men (with perpetrator questions) using the same broad questions; for example, the question above 'have you ever been in a situation where a man obtained sexual acts with you, such as anal or oral intercourse when you didn't want to by using threats or physical force?' was asked in this way in the female version of the survey but in the male version the question was 'have you ever been in a situation where you obtained sexual acts with a woman, such as anal or oral intercourse when she didn't want to by using threats or physical force?'

Another scale which has been used widely in violence and abuse research is the Conflict Tactics Scale (Straus, 1979). This scale lists a number of examples of different behaviours and asks respondents about their experiences in a range of contexts. The questions therefore focus on a range of behaviours. Although this scale is widely used in violence against women research, it is not without its limitations. As Walby and Towers (2017, p. 20) explain, 'The definition of violence and the distinction between different types is not anchored in the criminal or other bodies of law, but rather in a modified version of the Conflict Tactics Scale.' The Conflict Tactics Scale focuses on the actions of the perpetrator rather than the harm to the victim, which is problematic as it assumes the same level of harm always emerges from a given action. It also includes some actions where there was no intention to cause harm. Walby (2007, p. 17) raises concern that the CTS 'produces spurious gender symmetry,' that is, it produces results which suggest that there are no gender differences in the use of violence. According to Walby, this can be explained by at least three factors, including:

> the exclusion of sexual violence and stalking; the significance of meaning and context; the lack of congruency of behavioural actions with impact on the victim. This criticism has several overlapping aspects. One is a preference for differentiating the intentions behind the action; it may be an initiation of aggression, or retaliation in response, or self-defence.
>
> (Walby, 2007, p. 17)

Walby et al. (2017, pp. 159-160) propose that a single measurement framework should replace the existing myriad of approaches. They argue that the

> existing multiple measurement practices have developed relatively separately in relation to diverse relevant policy fields and are consequently embedded in disparate frameworks. Some of these policy fields are deeply sedimented in a range of specialised institutions.

Walby et al. (2017) suggest a number of core components critical to a single measurement framework, which include:

1   Actions (and intentions) AND harms (and non-consent)
2   Variations by types of violence
3   Gender dimensions which include the sex of victim and perpetrator, the relationship between victim and perpetrator, whether there was a sexual aspect to the violence as well as physical and whether there was a gender motivation.

They also highlight the need for harmonisation in terms of definition and counting, for example what takes precedence when there are multiple victims/perpetrators/crimes in the same event. This issue is discussed in the following section.

Counting violence against women

A further consideration in conducting prevalence survey research on gender, violence and abuse is what to count. Currently, there are two ways of counting: counting crimes and counting victimisation (Walby et al., 2016). The approach that is chosen will affect what can be said about the prevalence of violence against women. Counting crimes, the approach taken by most national victimisation surveys (for example the Crime Survey for England and Wales), works well when there is a single crime incident involving a single victim. However, one of the notable features of violence against women, especially domestic/intimate partner violence, is that it often involves repeat or multiple victimisation. It is well documented that women on average experience at least 35 incidents of domestic violence before reporting to the police. This poses difficulties in terms of capturing the true extent of victimisation. A counting crime approach would not capture the 35 incidents of violence; instead, it would capture this as a single crime. Take the following question as an example:

> Question: Have you experienced any form of physical violence or abuse by an intimate partner or ex-partner in the previous 12 months?

One participant may answer 'yes' and have experienced a single incident of violence over that period, whereas a second participant may answer 'yes' but have experienced multiple incidents of violence over the same period. This style of question therefore reduces the second participant's sustained experience of victimisation to one single event.

The alternative approach counts victimisation instead of crimes/incidents. This allows participants to provide more detail on their experiences of victimisation, and is not restricted to the measurement of incidents. Whilst on the surface this may seem straightforward, this approach also creates difficulties as it is not possible for most surveys to have an unlimited number of potential responses to a question. Consequently, the typical approach has been to ignore or 'cap' the frequency of victimisations of this group in order to avoid this problem. However, this has obvious problems with obtaining a true prevalence of victimisation, leading to what Walby et al. (2016, p. 1204) describe as 'a tension . . . between two goals: accurately assessing the year on year changes in the rate of crime and accurately reporting the extent and distribution of violent crime victimisation.'

Conducting surveys

Sampling

Once a survey has been designed, there are a number of further considerations relating to how the survey research is conducted. The first is sampling, the process of recruiting participants. A key consideration in participant sampling is the inclusion and exclusion criteria which define which individuals will be invited to take part. Some of these criteria will be dictated by the nature of the survey; for example, the NUS (2018) survey on staff-student sexual misconduct at UK universities sampled current and former students aged 16 and over. However, national/international standalone violence against women surveys, and crime surveys with violence against women questions, tend to following similar sampling approaches which can limit how representative the sample is of the population as a whole. In particular, these surveys are often limited to a specific age range, and exclude individuals who live in non-residential environments.

The extent to which the participant age range is limited depends on the individual survey; however, it is common for surveys to exclude children and older adults/the elderly. One of the most under-acknowledged limitations of the CSEW is the upper age limit of 59, which was placed on the intimate violence module when it was introduced in 2004. Although the general crime survey does not have this upper age limit, the intimate violence self-completion module, which collects specific information on sexual violence victimisation, has imposed a limit. The only justification for this is found in Walby and Allen's 2004 evaluation of the British Crime Survey (BCS; the predecessor to the CSEW):

> Although the BCS includes respondents aged 16 and over, the questions on interpersonal violence were only asked of those aged between 16 and 59. This was for two main reasons. First, older people have greater difficulty with or resistance to using a computer in this way. Secondly, it was thought that issues of elder abuse (from family members other than intimates) might get confused with responses about violence from intimates and that these issues were more appropriately dealt with in a specialised survey.
>
> (Walby and Allen, 2004, p. 118)

Whilst the Office of National Statistics (ONS) have now increased the age-cap to 74 years, effective from April 2017 (ONS, 2018), there remains a period of 13 years in which older women have been excluded from the intimate violence module of the CSEW. This has hindered understanding of the extent and nature of violence against older women. Moreover, those under the age of 16 are also not included in the survey, despite the fact that sexual violence against children is relatively common (Radford et al., 2013).

An additional problem with the sampling method employed by the CSEW is that it excludes people living in institutions including hospitals, care homes, prisons and other non-residential arrangements. Walby and Myhill (2001, p. 510) note this omission is particularly significant for surveys on violence against women because this group have a higher likelihood of being in temporary accommodation such as refuges, hostels, living with friends or relatives or in hotels/bed and breakfast accommodation. They argue,

It is precisely women who are in the immediate aftermath of a domestic assault who are more likely than the average woman to be living in such temporary accommodation.

The exclusion of people living in care homes from survey samples disproportionately affects those at the youngest and oldest ends of the age spectrum. The most recent data from the ONS reveals that 291,000 people aged 65 and over were living in residential care in 2011, and that of all the people living in residential care, 82.5 percent were over the age of 65 (ONS, 2014). Consequently, older people are disproportionately affected by the exclusion of participants in institutional settings by virtue of the fact that most people in these institutions are aged over 65.

Self-completion questionnaires or survey 'interviews'

In addition to the methodological issues common to all survey research (for example sampling, managing incomplete survey responses etc.), survey research which examines violence against women can face additional challenges. One of these challenges concerns the method by which the survey is administered. Surveys can be filled out by the participant themselves, either on paper, or more typically online. However, it is also possible to complete a survey via a 'survey interview' in which a researcher asks the survey questions and notes down the participant's responses. This latter method of survey completion can present particular problems for violence and abuse research. Specifically, victim-survivors of domestic and sexual violence may well be reluctant to reveal instances of abuse to an interviewer. Surveys conducted in respondents' homes must also take account of the presence of other household members during interviews, especially where this may have implications for the safety of the respondent (Mirrlees-Black, 1999).

The CSEW survey combines both 'survey interview' and self-report methods, with researchers interviewing one 'eligible' individual from each selected household. A face-to-face interview is used in the completion of the main survey, whilst self-completion is used for specific modules including the module covering intimate violence (domestic violence, sexual assault and stalking). The confidential nature of the self-completion methodology produces greater disclosure of intimate violence than does the face-to-face section of the survey. For example, it is estimated that the disclosure rate for domestic violent crime (violence against the person and sexual offences) is 3.8 times higher when measured via self-completion than when measured via the face-to-face method (Walby et al., 2016).

Academic researchers also utilise self-completion surveys to examine different forms of violence and abuse. In a recent study by Al-Modallal et al. (2015), self-completion surveys were used to examine experiences of intimate partner violence among 300 women in Jordan. The researchers recruited women who were visiting healthcare centres in Jordan and, after obtaining consent, provided women with questionnaires which they were then able to complete on their own (but whilst in the healthcare facility).

Using a survey as part of a comparative study: Has anything changed? Results of a comparative study (1977–2010) on opinions on rape

In 2010 one of the authors (Westmarland) worked as part of a team to conduct a comparative study about opinions on rape (Brown et al., 2010a). This coincided with being appointed as a team of academics to conduct a rapid evidence assessment to inform the Government's Stern Review on rape (see Brown et al., 2010b; Stern, 2010). One of the questions that the academics were briefed with answering was whether there was any evidence of changing attitudes to rape over time. It was difficult to answer this question with existing data, because although there had been a range of surveys asking about attitudes to rape, most of them had asked different questions or at least had used different wording to examine the same 'rape myths.' In addition, samples were often narrow, for example a sample might be comprised of university students rather than individuals drawn from the general population. The earliest survey on opinions on rape that was found was conducted on 1 July 1977 and published in the Daily Mail (it linked to a high-profile rape case where an 18 year old guardsman, Thomas Holdsworth, had had his three year custodial sentence for rape and assault reduced on appeal to a six-month sentence due to otherwise good behaviour and the court's perception that the victim was only severely injured because she had not 'submitted' to the rape).

In order to examine how attitudes to rape had changed since 1977, the academics decided to rerun the survey, collecting the 2010 data in as close a replication of the 1977 as possible. However, it was found that there were several places where amendments had to be made. One of the key challenges was making sure that the 2010 survey did not seem dated in terms of its language. The largest change that was made in this regard was the alteration of the regularly used term 'birching' as a punishment option in the 1977 survey to 'corporal punishment' in the 2010 survey. Hence, effort was made to keep the meaning of the original terms the same but to replace outdated words with modern words that would be understood by new readers. Other considerations included the fact that the original survey followed in the aftermath of a rape case that received a high degree of public interest (the Holdsworth case in 1977). Therefore, to bring some comparability of context, the 2010 survey was run soon after the publication of the Independent Police Complaints Committee's report on the case of John Worboys, known as the 'Black cab rapist.'

Another key change related to the introduction of male rape as a criminal offence in 1994; male rape which was not included in the 1977 survey as it was not considered to be a crime at that time. An additional question was added in to the 2010 survey which asked about what male respondents would do if faced with rape (the same wording as the question only asked of females in 1977). Finally, the biggest change was the mode of survey – in 1977 a face-to-face survey had been conducted (with 1,044 respondents), whilst in 2010 the survey was conducted online (with 2,057 respondents). Methodologically, this was not ideal. Previous research suggests that online surveys tend to generate more 'mid-range' responses (such as neither agree nor disagree) and greater use of the 'don't know' option (Duffy et al., 2005). The research team attempted to deal with this in the analyses by removing mid-range and 'don't know' responses from the data.

There were also differences in the two samples with regards to age and social class. In terms of age, there were fewer respondents aged 65 or older in the 1977 sample than in the 2010 sample (14 percent compared with 22 percent). This may be because of an ageing population generally and/or because older people have more time to participate in online surveys. In terms of social class, the 2010 sample contained more respondents in the upper middle and fewer in the lower middle social class than the 1977 sample. This may be due to increased affluence and/or because higher income groups have more access to the internet, as suggested by Duffy et al. (2005).

We did not write about the reasons behind their change of mode of survey in the final publication as it was a short (12-page) report intended to inform the Stern Review and related policy developments. However, the reasons for the change of mode were linked to cost (it is far more expensive to access respondents in person than online) and to ethics – it is now generally considered more difficult ethically to ask respondents in person about 'sensitive' issues such as sexual violence. Given that the survey also asked questions about how the participant themselves thought they would act if they were raped, for example whether they would 'fight back,' report to the police etc., it was decided that these questions would be too sensitive to ask in a face-to-face survey.

Overall, the study found that opinions on rape remain negative in some ways (e.g. that the law is unfair on rape victims and that many people would not report rape to the police). In other ways though the findings were optimistic (e.g. more people agreed in 2010 that rape is a serious crime, and there was less support for the opinion that if a woman gets raped it is usually her fault or the opinion that the prior sexual experience of the woman should be taken into consideration when punishing those found guilty of rape). Despite the fact that alterations to the survey method precluded direct comparisons between attitudes in 1977 and those in 2010, the authors were satisfied that the comparative study in its amended form was a useful tool in enabling them to answer the research question.

Using a telephone survey as part of a longitudinal quasi-experimental study

In Project Mirabal, one of the authors (Westmarland) worked with a team of researchers to design a longitudinal survey of the views of partners and ex-partners of men attending domestic violence perpetrator programmes (DVPPs). Women were asked to participate in five telephone surveys covering six-time points. The surveys were highly structured and coded, and even the language used in between sections was formulaic in nature, due to the number of researchers involved in administering the telephone survey. Participants were contacted every three months and asked about their partner or ex-partner's behaviour during that time. In total, 162 women took part in the first interview (100 in the intervention group and 62 in the comparison), and by the fifth interview this number had fallen to 128. Women who participated in the full set of five interviews were given £60 of high stress vouchers to compensate them for their time and to thank them for participating. Giving vouchers rather than cash as 'thank yous' meant that any participants who were receiving welfare benefits did not have to declare the money as income, something which could have created problems for their family income streams.

The survey provided valuable data to answer one of the project's key research objectives: to measure change amongst men on community based DVPPs. However, its aim to compare change for men on programmes with a matched comparison group was not successful. Attempts to run a quasi-experimental research design were hampered by the difficulty in obtaining a suitable comparison group. The researchers sought to compare the experiences of one group of women whose partners and ex-partners had attended a DVPP with a group of women whose partners had not attended one, and for whom there was not one available in their locality (so it was not simply that the men had not volunteered to attend a programme). Whilst it might have been possible to obtain a comparison sample from refuge populations, it was decided that women in refuges were unlikely to represent an adequate comparison group to the partners or ex-partners of men attending a perpetrator programme. Instead, the comparison group was drawn from community support groups – primarily through a structured support group called the Freedom Programme.

However, it was found that the samples of women were too different to allow comparisons to be drawn between the two groups. The women in the comparison group were much more likely to have children who had no contact at all with their father than the women in the intervention group. In addition, the two groups differed in the reason behind this lack of paternal contact; in the comparison group it was most often because the perpetrator did not want contact, whereas in the intervention group it was more likely to be due to decisions made by the family court. However, the biggest difference between the two groups was in relation to continued relationships. In the intervention group nearly half of the women were in a relationship with the man before he started on a programme, and over a third were still in this relationship 15 months later. In contrast, only 13 percent of the women in the comparison group were in a relationship with the perpetrator at the time of the first interview, with nine percent still in the relationship 15 months later. It may have been possible to control for these differences with larger sample sizes, but studies of this nature do not tend to recruit the numbers that would have been required.

Following Kelly et al. (2013), it was concluded that developing appropriate comparison or control groups in violence against women research unfortunately remains methodologically problematic. The survey therefore worked well in terms of its longitudinal element, but poorly in terms of its quasi-experimental design. As time went on, the importance of the relatively large longitudinal qualitative interview sample (64 men and 48 women) gained more prominence, and it became clear that even a larger sample of quantitative surveys would not have been as useful in answering the overall research questions as the qualitative data was.

Summary

This chapter has described some of the issues that can arise when designing and conducting surveys on gender, violence and abuse. It has drawn on particular examples of where this method has been used, highlighted different approaches to address some of the primary concerns in using this method and offered practical tips based on techniques that have worked well in our own research and that of others.

References

Al-Modallal, H., Abu Zayed, I., Abujilban, S., Shehab, T. and Atoum, M. (2015) Prevalence of intimate partner violence among women visiting health care centers in Palestine refugee camps in Jordan, *Health Care for Women International, 36*(2), pp. 137-148.

Brown, J., Horvath, M., Kelly, L. and Westmarland, N. (2010a) *Has Anything Changed? Results of a Comparative Study (1977-2010) on Opinions on Rape*. London: Government Equalities Office.

Brown, J., Horvath, M., Kelly, L. and Westmarland, N. (2010b) *Connections and Disconnections: Assessing Evidence, Knowledge and Practice in Responses to Rape*. London: Government Equalities Office.

Duffy, B., Smith, K., Terhanian, G. and Bremer, J. (2005) Comparing data from online and face-to-face surveys, *International Journal of Market Research, 47*(6), pp. 615-639.

Fisher, B. S. (2009) The effects of survey question wording on rape estimates: Evidence from a quasi-experimental design, *Violence against Women, 15*(2), pp. 133-147.

Hagemann-White, C. (2001) European research on the prevalence of violence against women, *Violence against Women, 7*(7), pp. 732-759.

HMIC (2014) *Crime-Recording: Making the Victim Count: The Final Report of an Inspection of Crime Data Integrity in Police Forces in England and Wales*. London: Her Majesty's Inspectorate of Constabulary.

Hough, J. M. and Mayhew, P. (1983) *The British Crime Survey*. Home Office Research Study 76. London: Her Majesty's Stationary Office.

Johnson, S. M., Murphy, M. J. and Gidycz, C. A. (2017) Reliability and validity of the sexual experiences survey-short forms victimization and perpetration, *Violence and Victims, 32*(1), pp. 78-92.

Kelly, L., Adler, J. A., Horvath, M. A. H., Lovett, J., Coulson, M., Kernohan, D. and Gray, M. (2013) *Evaluation of the Pilot of Domestic Violence Protection Orders*. Home Office Research Report 76. London: Home Office.

Koss, M. P., Gidycz, C. A. and Wisniewski, N. (1987) The scope of rape: Incidence and prevalence of sexual aggression and victimization in a national sample of higher education students. *Journal of Consulting and Clinical Psychology, 55*(2), pp. 162-170.

Lees, S. (1996) Unreasonable doubt: the outcomes of rape trials, In: M. Hester, L. Kelly and J. Radford (Eds.) *Women, Violence and Male Power* (pp. 99-129). Milton Keynes: Open University Press.

McGlynn, C. and Rackley, E. (2018) Why 'upskirting' needs to be made a sex crime, *The Conversation*, 15 August [Online]. Available at: https://theconversation.com/why-upskirting-needs-to-be-made-a-sex-crime-82357 (Accessed: 21 June 2018).

Ministry of Justice (2013) *An Overview of Sexual Offending in England and Wales, Statistics Bulletin*. London: Ministry of Justice, Home Office and the Office for National Statistics.

Mirrlees-Black, C. (1999) *Domestic Violence: Findings from a New British Crime Survey Self-Completion Questionnaire*. London: Home Office.

Müller, U., Schröttle, M. and Glammeier, S. (2003) *Health, Well-Being and Personal Safety of Women in Germany: A Representative Study of Violence against Women in Germany*. Berlin: Federal Ministry for Family Affairs, Senior Citizens, Women and Youth.

Myhill, A. (2017) Measuring domestic violence: Context is everything, *Journal of Gender-Based Violence, 1*(1), pp. 33-44.

Nguyen, K. H., Kress, H., Atuchukwu, V., Onotu, D., Swaminathan, M., Ogbanufe, O., Msungama, W. and Sumner, S. A. (2018) Disclosure of sexual violence among girls and young women aged 13 to 24 years: Results from the violence against children surveys in Nigeria and Malawi, *Journal of Interpersonal Violence*, Epub ahead of print 15 February 2018. DOI: 10.1177/0886260518757225.

Office for National Statistics (2014) *Changes in the Older Resident Care Home Population between 2001 and 2011*. London: Office for National Statistics.

Office for National Statistics (2018) *Methodology: Improving Crime Statistics for England and Wales - Progress Update July 2018. Latest Update on the Progress Being Made to Improve Crime Statistics for England and Wales*. Available from: https://www.ons.gov.uk/peoplepopulationandcommunity/crimeandjustice/methodologies/improvingcrimestatisticsforenglandandwalesprogressupdate

Percy, A. and Mayhew, P. (1997) Estimating sexual victimisation in a national crime survey: A new approach, *Studies on Crime and Crime Prevention*, 6(2), pp. 125–150.

Radford, L., Corral, S., Bradley, C. and Fisher, H. L. (2013) The prevalence and impact of child maltreatment and other types of victimization in the UK: Findings from a population survey or caregivers, children and young people and young adults, *Child Abuse & Neglect*, 37(10), pp. 801–813.

Sarantakos, S. (2012) *Social Research*, 3rd ed. London: Palgrave.

Stern, V. (2010) The Stern Review: A Report by Baroness Vivien Stern CBE of an Independent Review into How Rape Complaints Are Handled by Public Authorities In England and Wales. *London: Government Equalities Office/Home Office*.

Straus, M. A. (1979). Measuring intrafamily conflict and violence: The conflict tactics (CT) scales, *Journal of Marriage and the Family*, 41(1), 75–88.

Tolman, D. L. and Szalacha, L. A. (1999) Dimensions of desire, *Psychology of Women Quarterly*, 23(1), pp. 7–39.

Walby, S. (2007) *Indicators to Measure Violence against Women: Invited Paper*, Expert Group Meeting on Indicators to Measure Violence against Women. Geneva: United Nations Statistical Commission and Economic Commission for Europe, 8–10 October.

Walby, S. and Allen, J. (2004) *Domestic Violence, Sexual Assault and Stalking: Findings from the British Crime Survey*. Home Office Research Study 279. London: Home Office.

Walby, S. and Myhill, A. (2001) New survey methodologies in researching violence against women, *British Journal of Criminology*, 41(3), pp. 502–522.

Walby, S. and Towers, J. (2017) Measuring violence to end violence: Mainstreaming gender, *Journal of Gender-Based Violence*, 1(1), pp. 11–31.

Walby, S., Towers, J., Balderston, S., Corradi, C., Francis, B., Heiskanen, M., Helweg-Larsen, K., Mergaert, L., Olive, P., Palmer, E., Stöckl, H. and Strid, S. (2017) *The Concept and Measurement of Violence against Women and Men*. Bristol: Policy Press.

Walby, S., Towers, J. and Francis, B. (2016) Is violent crime increasing or decreasing? A new methodology to measure repeat attacks making visible the significance of gender and domestic relations, *British Journal of Criminology*, 56(6), pp. 1203–1234.

7 Arts-based and creative methods

Alongside the more developed and well-known qualitative research methods such as interviews, feminist researchers are increasingly using arts-based and other creative methods to explore gender, violence and abuse – usually as part of a participatory action research approach. Arts-based research is defined as 'research that uses the arts, in the broadest sense, to explore, understand, represent and even challenge human action and experience' (Savin-Baden and Wimpenny, 2014, p. 1). Arts-based methods can be used both along and alongside more traditional methods. The terms 'arts-based methods' and 'arts-based research' are broad umbrella terms that refer to a range of methods and approaches. According to Wang et al. (2017), arts-based methods draw on a range of techniques including writing, music, performance, dance, visual art, film and other mediums. Representational forms include but are not limited to short narratives, novels, experimental writing, poems, collages, paintings, drawings, performance scripts, theatre performances, dances, documentaries and songs. This genre of methods also comprises new theoretical and epistemological groundings that are significantly expanding qualitative inquiry.

Sinner et al. (2006) trace the emergence of arts-based research methods to the 1970s, with arts-based practices emerging as a distinct methodological inquiry in the 1990s. They identify that this incorporation of arts-based methods is in part a result of advances in arts-based therapies. Healthcare researchers, special education researchers, psychologists and others have increasingly turned to the arts for their therapeutic, restorative and empowering qualities. Although there are differences between therapeutic practices and research practices, the work of these practitioners is cited throughout this text, as there is no doubt that knowledge derived from the practices of arts-based therapies has informed our understanding of arts-based research practices.

Coemans et al. (2015) note that arts-based methods have generally been applied either as a data collection technique or as a dissemination technique.

In the former, arts-based methods are considered research in their own right. Examples include sculptures, drawings or collages which replace other qualitative methods of data collection, such as interviews. The art is used as a medium which 'allows participants to communicate with researchers about their experiences and perceptions' (Coemans et al., 2015, p. 34). In the latter, arts-based methods are used to translate research findings, replacing more traditional dissemination vehicles such as written reports, briefing notes or books. A range of arts-based methods can be used to achieve this, including collage, sculptures, photos, videos, dance or drama.

Regardless of the specific tools used, researchers use arts-based methods to address specific methodological problems, often taking a participatory action research approach. This approach involves carrying out research in collaboration with those engaged in the practice that is being studied (Bergold and Thomas, 2012). Arts-based methods are seen as being particularly appropriate for accessing knowledge which is not easily expressed in words, or with participants for whom words or language are difficult (Tarr et al., 2018). This includes, but is not limited to, children and young people, those who speak a different language to the researcher and also those who find speaking or writing about their experiences traumatic. Arts-based methods have also been identified as ideally suited to gender, violence and abuse research (Clover, 2011), examples of which are addressed within this chapter. However, it is also important to be aware of the challenges that can arise when working with these methods. To this end, this chapter describes some of the most commonly used arts-based methods and gives examples of these, before considering some of the associated challenges.

Visual methods

One category of arts-based research is visual methods, incorporating photos, videos, artwork and other images. Although these are not the only form of arts-based method, they are probably the most commonly used, and we found more examples of this than other arts-based methods when conducting research for this book. Hence, most of the examples included in this chapter use some form of visual method to research gender, violence and abuse.

Pauwels (2010) has argued that visual research as a methodological genre is ill-defined and lacks a unified conceptual and methodological framework. Despite this lack of clarity, visual methods have a long history of application across the social sciences. Although originally rooted in anthropology, these methods are now popular within sociology, criminology, other social sciences, education and health (Wiles et al., 2008). As Balomenou and Garrod (2016,

p. 335) note, 'Although it is often thought of as a new technique, participant-generated image (PGI) research has a track record of application across the social sciences reaching back to the 1970s.'

It is argued that visual methods provide participants with a greater level of autonomy and the ability to express concepts, feelings or ideas that would not necessarily be possible using traditional qualitative interview methods (Stedman et al., 2004). Kanyeredzi et al. (2014, p. 165) suggest,

> When visual approaches are used in the social sciences, the distinction between researcher and researched becomes destabilized, due to a greater transference of autonomy and narrative authority over to the participant who creates, organizes and analyses data in partnership with the researcher.

Kanyeredzi et al. further state that visual methods can be particularly useful in research that seeks to engage with groups that are perceived to be 'hard-to reach.' They argue,

> Visual researchers, especially those interested in examining "experience" have found merit in using visual methods to access "hard to reach" issues, such as the environmental spaces that individuals experientially inhabit and the emotional and embodied elements of experience that are always present, but rarely directly acknowledged in qualitative research.
>
> (Kanyeredzi et al., 2014, p. 16)

One of the most commonly used visual methods involves the collection of participant-generated imagery. This encompasses both photovoice (a term first coined in the late 1990s according to Coemans et al., 2017), which involves participants taking their own photos and then discussing them with the researcher(s), and photo elicitation, which involves the use of images as stimuli for interviews or focus group discussions (Harper, 2012). It has been argued that participant-generated images (photovoice) give agency and voice to previously silenced populations, their lives and the environments in which they live (Frohmann, 2005). Perhaps because of this, photovoice has been identified as method particularly suited to feminist research, with Wang and Burris (1997) arguing that it can be used to conduct research *by* and *with* women, rather than *on* or *of* women.

Using photography to understand women's experiences of domestic violence

A study by Frohmann (2005) used photography and narrative to examine women's experiences of domestic violence, particularly their strategies for living and coping with violence in their lives. The Framing Safety Project comprised three components: self-exploration, reflection and change; community education – social action; and research. Frohmann states that the project was designed to be

> a therapeutic tool, a community education and action strategy, participatory action research for women to explore their experiences living in and extricating themselves from a battering relationship, and a means of informing others about the realities of these experiences.
>
> (Frohmann, 2005, p. 1397)

The project was rooted within a feminist methodological framework. Frohmann argued that the use of photovoice empowered women in the research process by giving them autonomy over which images were taken and used. As Frohmann states,

> This method gives women a medium to frame and define what is significant in a specific setting and within the larger context of social relationships and the environments in which they live. They choose the subjects of the photographs. They determine who or what to include or exclude from the frames.
>
> (Frohmann, 2005, p. 1400)

Over a period of 4–5 weeks, 29 women participants took between five and seven photos each week. These photos were then discussed in group and individual interviews and discussions, with a particular focus on why they took those particular photos, how they categorised the photo on a safety-danger continuum and which photos they didn't take and why. Frohmann (2005) comments that the photographs taken by the women conveyed the complexity of their lives. She notes that several of the women had taken similar photographs and/or commented that others' photographs represented an aspect of their own lives.

Photography is often used alongside other methods to examine lived experiences. These other methods can include additional arts-based methods or more traditional quantitative or qualitative methods. One of the benefits of using multiple methods (mixed methods) within research is the ability to explore experiences from different angles using different methods.

Using photography to explore African and Caribbean heritage women's experiences

For her doctoral research, Kanyeredzi (2014) examined the lived experiences of violence and abuse amongst African and Caribbean heritage women living in the UK. Specifically, she focused on the women's help seeking and the consequences of the violence for their bodies and mental well-being. The study took a mixed methods approach, and involved biographical interviews alongside photo elicitation, phot production and map-based methods. Nine victim-survivors were interviewed over a two or three-stage life history process. They used existing photographs (photo elicitation) to share their experiences of violence as well as photographs they created as part of the research process (photo production) to discuss the places, spaces and objects of importance to them. All of the women had experienced emotional abuse and some had also experienced sexual violence and physical violence, either as children and/or as adults in intimate relationships. In addition, several of the women had experienced racism.

Kanyeredzi used the first interview with each participant to focus on events in their life, their background and what being a Black woman meant to them. She remarks that one participant narrated her life story from a single opening question of *'Can you tell me a bit about yourself?'* (Kanyeredzi, 2014, p. 67). Women were asked to bring along personal photographs to the first or second interviews. This resulted in highly participatory interviews in which the women spoke about their choice of photographs, what the photographs depicted and why they were important to them. Whilst Kanyeredzi did not directly ask about the women's experiences of violence and abuse in the initial phase of the interviews, she found that the women often elected to bring these topics into discussion fairly early on. In some cases women brought along the participant recruitment poster with annotated ticks against the violence and abuse that they had experienced. Kanyeredzi notes that her approach of taking the women's lead in addressing the topic of violence and abuse early on seemed to provide a sense of relief for participants, such that the 'worst part was over' (Kanyeredzi, 2014, p. 67). This allowed the participants to relax more into the conversation as it moved on to wider topics. In the later interviews, women were invited to use disposable cameras or their own camera phones to take new photos of objects, spaces or places that were important to them. Kanyeredzi found that these newly created photos and the narrative explorations gave her a sense of 'having walked alongside each woman for a brief moment in their lives' (Kanyeredzi, 2014, p. 70). In this sense, she concluded that the use of photography, both existing and newly produced, had led to her being able to pursue ideas and themes with the women that would not have been possible through solely narrative based interviews.

Reflecting on the use of photos in research, Kanyeredzi et al. (2014) liken the use of photographs to making a patchwork quilt. They describe how

> each woman created a show, stitch and tell where she chose where to begin, where to pause and where to continue. The women used the photographs they created to re-focus the researcher's attention to earlier points in their narratives that might have been either too painful, clumsy or required further

explication. Once the women took the researcher back to that point in the story, they used the photographs to stitch in the details.

(Kanyeredzi et al., 2014, p. 172)

The use of photographs therefore prompted the women to recollect details of their stories, providing them with a way to provide more depth to their experiences. The two/three life history interview process used in the research was intended to give women the time and space to build trust with the researcher, reflect on what they had said and clarify earlier points. At the second or third interview, women were asked how they felt after the first interview and during the interim. The authors explain,

> Looking creates affect, new ways of understanding for the participant and for the researcher. Looking at photographs prompted the women to further recollect details about their stories, offer new reflections about the recollection, or in many cases disclose another story of abuse or violence and its legacies, inviting the researcher to explore these avenues further. The women used the photographs of the past and those they created to stitch together the nuances of the present, past and future directions of their quilts.
>
> (Kanyeredzi et al., 2014, p. 174)

Using cartoon-based research 'workbooks' with children

Arts-based methods that utilise drawing can be particularly useful in research with children (Bradbury-Jones and Taylor, 2015), and have long been used in research examining sensitive topics such as the experience of living in care (Coholic et al., 2009). Such methods are seen as useful in giving children a 'voice' compared with other methods which either exclude children or limit their ability to participate in research (Mand, 2012). These methods have also been used in research with children on the topic of domestic violence.

In her doctoral study examining the impact of domestic violence perpetrator programmes on children and young people, Alderson (supervised by Westmarland) used 'research workbooks' with children alongside interviews. Drawing on work from previous researchers (McSherry et al., 2008) the research workbook, titled 'The Life Story Book,' was used with children to collect information about their perceptions of their father/father figures' participation in a domestic violence perpetrator progamme. This workbook was chosen as it was sensitive enough to allow children to speak about this difficult topic and it fitted within the overarching feminist framework of the project.

Alderson (2015) describes the research workbook as including a variety of tasks that children would find fun to do and could complete whilst talking about their experiences. The tasks were designed in a question and answer format; the first three questions were about the child's age, their favourite TV programme and the person they would most like to be. These opening questions facilitated rapport and the development of trust between Alderson and the children. Following these ice-breaker questions, there was space for children to draw a picture of themselves. Particular care was taken to position each of the task-based questions sequentially within the research workbook (easier questions first) to encourage children to feel comfortable, and each topic or question was made broad enough to allow the child to talk freely about a particular issue. The draw and write tasks within the research workbook included picture drawing, letter writing, Likert type scales, smiley faces and comparing family activities before and after their father's participation on a domestic violence perpetrator programme. The remaining tasks within the research book addressed more personal issues, including family members or friends the child could talk to; activities the child did with their father; safety levels (depicted by a ladder); and their feelings around their father. As such, the research workbook was used as a facilitative method for verbal communication rather than as a direct examination of the meaning of the children's drawings or other completed tasks.

Children's workers and staff working on local community based domestic violence projects helped guide the development of the research workbooks, providing information and direction on appropriate types of questions and language. The workbooks were viewed as suitable for research with children given the limited verbal ability of young children. The workbooks included drawing activities and other tasks which helped to maintain concentration levels and provided children with the opportunity to share feelings and thoughts without using words or other verbal communication. This approach was also viewed as less threatening for children. The drawings in the research book were not intended to be used as a way of diagnosing children, or as a therapeutic tool, but rather as an opportunity for the children to talk about what they had drawn and for the researcher to ask the children questions about the drawings.

Story-based methods

Hargreaves (2015) considers how story-based methods have been used to investigate violence against Indigenous women in Canada. In particular, she writes about how documentary maker Christine Welsh used storytelling practices as a form of knowledge making in her documentary film *Finding Dawn*. Dawn Crey's remains were found at Pickton farm, along with the remains of many other women. In Welsh's *Finding Dawn*, Dawn's story is told in a manner which reaches beyond the simplistic way in which such stories had been previously presented in the media. Rather than pathologising the women as isolated, victimised fig-ures, Hargreaves notes that *Finding Dawn* situates the murder of Dawn Crey as part of a larger picture of gendered racism and colonial social suffering.

Hargreaves argues that by using storytelling, Welsh's documentary asserts the sovereignty of Indigenous frameworks of knowing. This approach can act as a counterpoint to statistical reports and government sponsored reports – highlighting that the many realities that 'facts' alone cannot tell us:

> The numbers alone cannot impart how a history (and present) of colonial displacement could make possible such unfathomable violence [and] how the terms on which we seek and make knowledge of this history impact how we conceive of its transformation.
>
> (Hargreaves, 2015, p. 94)

Hargreaves calls this 'survivance storywork' – a balanced account which docu-ments the real lived harms of colonial violence without feeding into the myth that Indigenous peoples are in need of 'rescue.' One of the important parts of the storytelling, Hargreaves argues, is the depiction of the annual remembrance walks for the missing and murdered which takes part every year in Vancouver. This, Hargreaves argues, forms a 'critical remembrance' as it demonstrates a form of resistance:

> Walking is shown as a strategic political expression and as a form of knowl-edge making that connects the strategies of research and remembrance employed in the DTES [Downtown East Side Vancouver] and along the High-way of Tears; it serves not merely as a way to mark a passing or to docu-ment discreet instances of disappearance and "demise." Drawing from Indig-enous traditions of social movement, *Finding Dawn* frames walking as a kind of "community procession" (to use Leanne Simpson's phrase), as a kind of mobilization that takes place over time and space.
>
> (Hargreaves, 2015, pp. 103–104)

Walking and storytelling as a form of political resistance was also used by O'Neill and Stenning (2014). They used story walks to explore what 'community' meant in the lives of residents from Downtown East Side (DTES) Vancouver. The story walks combined walking and storytelling with photography, and the method was developed by the researchers as a way of promoting inclusion in terms of how knowledge and public policy is developed. Like Hargreaves, O'Neill and Sten-ning sought to use a creative research method to offer a critical juxtaposition to the mainstream media's simplified and distorted portrayal of these residents as a 'problem' population who were only to be examined through the lenses of criminality, welfare or poverty. Walking, O'Neill and Stenning argue, is far more than getting from one place to another – it is also integral to how we perceive an environment and connect and communicate with others. They concluded that using story walks enabled people to tell their stories about how they came to live in DTES, how they negotiated their environment, how they kept safe, the importance of resistance and resilience and the struggle for recognition.

Storytelling and walking have been identified as particularly important arts-based research methods as they allow women's voices to be heard and allow for the (re)framing of these voices as purveyors of resistance as well as remembrance.

The creation and/or use of artefacts

Other arts-based methods that involve making items such as jewellery, pottery, sculptures and patchworks or quilts have also been used to explore experiences of violence and abuse. An arts-based, participant led workshop methodology was used by Recchia and McGarry (2017) to examine survivor's experiences and the impact of female genital mutilation (FGM). The workshop encompassed two strands: the creation of a persona and the sharing of artefacts. The creation of a persona involved the researcher, at the beginning of the workshop, lying on a sheet of paper and inviting a member of the workshop group to draw around her body. The resulting outline shape was used to represent a survivor of FGM. The outline was given the name Janet (this name was chosen by, but separate to, the names of the women in the workshop). This symbolic woman was then discussed in terms of her experiences of health services, her support needs and what professionals needed to know in order to properly support her.

The second element of the workshop involved artefacts. The women were invited to bring personal artefacts to the workshop or use some of the art materials provided at the workshop to create an artefact (made from pottery) that they could use to talk about themselves and their experiences. One example of an artefact made in the workshop was a pestle and mortar. The participant used this to explain her experience of FGM; the pestle represented the man's penis and the pounding of the pestle into the mortar was used as a way of representing the pain and trauma associated with sexual intercourse. Another woman made a mat, knife and bracelet to express her experience of FGM: the mat represented the place the FGM procedure was carried out, the knife was the tool used to perform FGM and the bracelet was the gift given to her after the procedure. In addition to the narratives captured by women describing their experiences through the artefacts, photos were taken of the final pottery models. These were then interpreted as findings in their own right.

This example demonstrates the ways arts-based methods can be used to not only generate data, but also as a prompt/tool to help facilitate discussion. Equally, the outputs of this kind of research can also be used to showcase research findings; for example at conferences or research workshops.

Anticipating and working with challenges associated with arts-based methods

This chapter has sought to showcase some of the innovative work that has been developed using arts-based methods. Perhaps in an attempt to move such methods out of the margins and into the mainstream, the challenges associated with these techniques have not been well documented in the literature. However, some discussion of these issues can be found in Brady and Brown's (2013) article. In this article, they use their research (which used storyboards, storybooklets and digital stories with young mothers) to show that whilst arts-based approaches can be rewarding for both participants and researchers, they can also give rise to a number of tensions and challenges. In particular, they raise the ethical issues associated with visual methods – highlighting that such methods serve to capture personal images and stories for 'time immemorial' (Brady and Brown, 2013, p. 102). This is particularly problematic in relation to work which aims to produce resources that may be used long into the future. Discussing their work with young mothers, Brady and Brown (2013) raise a number of potential concerns, including whether the participants are aware that their images may continue to be used after the project, whether artefacts should be destroyed after a number of years just as other data would be, whether the participants are still proud of their involvement and whether the long-term implications have been fully considered. These concerns become especially important when working with resources produced by participants who had experienced sexual intercourse that was forced or coerced. In these cases, the researchers were more careful about checking and double checking with participants about which parts of their resources could be used. However, even this came with its challenges, with the researchers also not wanting to go too far in removing such images:

> We questioned whether we were being over-protective to the point of denying agency or whether, as experienced researchers, we should be prepared to make some difficult decisions.
>
> (Brady and Brown, 2013, p. 104)

In these cases, they highlight that it was not only necessary to consider the wider context in terms of the participant herself, but also in terms of her child.

A quote from an interview can be anonymised, yet this is (more) difficult when working with photography used to tell individual stories. As additional notes of caution, the researchers warn that the circumstances of participants change over time – relationships may end, and people who are captured in the images may die. When looking at arts-based methods from a cautionary perspective, the researchers argue that 'such methods are not simply about "giving young people a voice"' (Brady and Brown, 2013, p. 108) which is presented without due consideration. Rather, they conclude that 'critical reflection by researchers is fundamental' (Brady and Brown, 2013, p. 108), that consent must be seen as a process not as a one-off consideration and that attention must be given to the outputs as well as the research process.

Summary

Arts-based and creative methods are umbrella terms that encompass a range of methods. Some of the most common approaches utilise either photos or arts and crafts, used either as standalone methods or in combination with other qualitative or quantitative methods. These approaches can be used to generate data in their own right, as a way of stimulating discussion and as outputs, for example photographs can be presented during workshops or conferences. It has been argued that arts-based and creative methods are particularly well suited to gender, violence and abuse research, especially when working with partici-pants who are deemed 'hard-to-reach,' or when researching topics said to be 'sensitive,' such as FGM. Arts-based methods represent a core component of participatory research, as they support a level of participant involvement which often reaches beyond that associated with more traditional research methods. Furthermore, it has been suggested these methods help to reduce (though not eliminate) the hierarchy between researcher and participant, a core commit-ment of feminist research. As shown in this chapter, arts-based methods can be used highly effectively within gender, violence and abuse research, especially in contexts where oral, or written, language may not be possible or appropriate.

References

Alderson, S. (2015) *An Investigation into the Impact of Domestic Violence Perpetrator Programmes on Children and Young People.* Durham e-Theses. Durham: Durham University.

Balomenou, N. and Garrod, B. (2016) A review of participant-generated image methods in the social sciences, *Journal of Mixed Methods Research, 10*(4), pp. 225–251.

Bergold, J. and Thomas, S. (2012) Participatory research methods: A methodological approach in motion, *Forum: Qualitative Social Research, 13*(1), Art. 30.

Bradbury-Jones, C. and Taylor, J. (2015) Engaging with children as co-researchers: Challenges, counter-challenges and solutions, *International Journal of Social Research Methodology*, *18*(2), pp. 161-173.

Brady, G. and Brown, G. (2013) Rewarding but let's talk about the challenges: Using arts based methods in research with young mothers, *Methodological Innovations Online*, *8*(1), pp. 99-112.

Clover, D. (2011) Successes and challenges of feminist arts-based participatory methodologies with homeless/street-involved women in Victoria, *Action Research*, *9*(1), pp. 12-26.

Coemans, S., Raymakers, A. L., Vandenabeele, J. and Hannes, K. (2017) Evaluating the extent to which social researchers apply feminist and empowerment frameworks in photovoice studies with female participants: A literature review, *Qualitative Social Work*, Epub ahead of print 27 April 2017. DOI: 10.1177/1473325017699263.

Coemans, S., Wang, Q., Leysen, J. and Hannes, K. (2015) The use of arts-based methods in community-based research with vulnerable populations: Protocol for a scoping review, *International Journal of Educational Research*, *71*, pp. 33-39.

Coholic, D., Lougheed, S. and Cadell, S. (2009) Exploring the helpfulness of arts-based methods with children living in foster care, *Traumatology*, *15*(3), pp. 64-71.

Frohmann, L. (2005) The framing safety project: Photographs and narratives by battered women, *Violence against Women*, *11*(11), pp. 1396-1419.

Hargreaves, A. (2015) Finding Dawn and missing women in Canada: Story-based methods in antiviolence research and remembrance, *Studies in American Indian Literatures*, *27*(3), pp. 82-111.

Harper, D. (2012) *Visual Sociology*. New York, NY: Routledge.

Kanyeredzi, A. (2014) *Knowing What I Know Now: Black Women Talk about Violence Inside and Outside of the Home*. Doctoral Thesis, London: London Metropolitan University.

Kanyeredzi, A., Reavey, P. and Brown, S. D. (2014) The role of the visual in narratives of violence: Co-creating fissures, In: Y. Taylor (Ed.) *The Entrepreneurial University: Engaging Publics, Intersecting Impacts* (pp. 165-184). Basingstoke: Palgrave MacMillan.

Mand, K. (2012) Giving children a 'voice': Arts-based participatory research activities and representation, *International Journal of Social Research Methodology*, *15*(2), pp. 149-160.

McSherry, D., Larkin, E., Fargas, M., Kelly, G., Robinson, C., McDonald, G., Schubotz, D. and Kilpatrick, R. (2008) *From Care to Where? A Care Pathways and Outcomes Report for Practitioners*. Belfast: Institute of Child care Research, Queens University.

O'Neill, M. and Stenning, P. (2014) Walking biographies and innovations in visual and participatory methods: Community, politics and resistance in downtown East Side Vancouver, In: C. Heinz and G. Hornung (Eds.) *The Medialization of Auto/Biographies: Different Forms and Their Communicative Contexts* (pp. 215-246). Hamburg: UVK.

Pauwels, L. (2010) Visual sociology reframed: An analytical synthesis and discussion of visual methods in social and cultural research, *Sociological Methods and Research*, *38*(4), pp. 545-581.

Recchia, N. and McGarry, J. (2017) 'Don't judge me': Narratives of living with FGM, *International Journal of Human Rights in Healthcare*, *10*(1), pp. 4-13.

Savin-Baden, M. and Wimpenny, K. (2014) *A Practical Guide to Arts-Related Research*. Rotterdam: Sense Publishers.

Sinner, A., Leggo, C., Irwin, R. L., Gouzouasis, P. and Grauer, K. (2006) Arts-based educational research dissertations: Reviewing the practices of new scholars, *Canadian Journal of Education*, *29*(4), pp. 1223-1270.

Stedman, R., Beckley, T., Wallace, S. and Ambard, M. (2004) A picture and 1000 words: Using resident-employed photography to understand attachment to high amenity places, *Journal of Leisure Research*, *36*(4), pp. 580-606.

Tarr, J., Gonzalez-Polledo, E. and Cornish, F. (2018) On liveness: Using arts workshops as a research method, *Qualitative Research*, *18*(1), pp. 36-52.

Wang, C. and Burris, M. A. (1997) Photovoice: Concept, methodology, and use for participatory needs assessment, *Health Education and Behavior*, *24*(3), pp. 369–387.

Wang, Q., Coemans, S., Siegesmund, R. and Hannes, K. (2017) Arts-based methods in socially engaged research practice: A classification framework, *Art Research International*, *2*(2), pp. 5–39.

Wiles, R., Prosser, J., Bagnoli, A., Clark, A., Davies, K., Holland, S. and Renold, E. (2008) *Visual Ethics: Ethical Issues in Visual Research*. ESRC National Centre for Research Methods Review Paper. Southampton: National Centre for Research Methods.

8 Working with existing data

Introduction

Whilst much gender, violence and abuse research involves primary, empirical research which generates new data, another approach involves analysis of existing data. There is increasing pressure by research funding bodies to make research data 'open access' and available to other researchers/the general public through data repositories. Similarly, researchers are being encouraged to use existing data to answer new research questions. This chapter will provide an overview of the different approaches to working with existing data, and will draw upon case studies to showcase the ways in which existing data have been used in recent gender, violence and abuse research.

Working with existing data

Working with existing data is a common approach in social research. Internationally, there have been various debates around research being 'open access,' whilst policy decisions by research councils, governments and public agencies have led to the creation of publically available data repositories which promote and facilitate the re-use of archived data. Against this background, the practice of carrying out new analyses with existing data is likely to increase. Examples of existing data repositories include the Global Health Observatory Data Repository, the UK Data Service (UKDS) and the Australian Data Archive. Increasingly, academics are encouraged (and sometimes required) to upload data from their research to repositories such as these. In the UK, the UKDS is funded by the Economic and Social Research Council (ESRC), although researchers who are unfunded, or funded by other organisations, can use the service and upload their data. As well as providing access to data sets uploaded to the repository, the UKDS also offers guidance and training on the use of data, develops best practice for data preservation and shares international expertise on the removal of barriers to data access.

A number of large data sets are available on the UKDS, including a data set from the European Union Agency for Fundamental Rights' (FRA) survey on violence against women (see Chapter 6), a data set from an ESRC funded study comparing love and domestic violence in heterosexual and same-sex relationships (Donovan and Hester, 2009) and a data set from a study examining intimate partner violence and women's employment in Tanzania (Watts and Vyas, 2010). Accessible data sets such as these provide researchers with the opportunity to conduct novel analysis on existing data as part of new research projects.

However, despite the growing surge in the use of existing data, there remains significant debate about whether the collection and/or analysis of existing data should be viewed as primary or secondary analysis. This is compounded by the inconsistency in terms used to describe such an approach. Cheng and Phillips (2014) highlight the confusion regarding the use of the terms 'primary' and 'secondary' to describe data and its analysis. They suggest that the source of this confusion lies in a lack of clarity regarding whether data employed in a given analysis should be considered 'primary data' or 'secondary data.' Some researchers and institutions/agencies will describe any original analysis conducted for the purpose of addressing new research questions as 'primary data analysis,' even if the data have been collected and analysed as part of a different, earlier research project (Cheng and Phillips, 2014). Others, however, would consider this latter scenario to be secondary analysis of existing data, as the data have been previously analysed, albeit for a different project and/or by different researchers. These researchers would only use the term 'primary data analysis' to describe the analysis of data collected by members of the research team. Cheng and Phillips (2014) suggest that the term 'secondary data analysis' should be avoided, as it does not accurately describe the process that is being carried out in the latter scenario.

To this end, this chapter uses the terminology 'analysis of existing data' to describe an original analysis of data which already exists for some other purpose (research or otherwise). Consequently, the term can be used to describe the analysis of data which has been collected by researchers or institutions to examine a prior research question, as in the scenario described above. However, the term can also be used to describe the analysis of data which existed prior to the commencement of the new research, but were not compiled for the purposes of a previous research study. For example, newspaper reports provide a source of existing data, but these data are compiled for journalistic purposes, not for research purposes.

Analysis of existing data

Cheng and Phillips (2014) suggest there are two approaches for analysing existing data: research question-driven and data-driven. In the first approach, researchers develop a hypothesis or question, and then find suitable existing data sets to address this question. In the latter approach, researchers examine existing data sets and decide what kinds of questions can be answered with the data. These approaches are often used in conjunction. Original analysis of existing data has been described as a 'cost-efficient way to make full use of data that are already collected to address potentially important new research questions or to provide a more nuanced assessment of the primary results from the original study' (Cheng and Phillips, p. 371).

Regardless of the terms adopted, it is important to acknowledge that analysis of existing data is not in itself a form of analysis, rather it describes the application of one or more analytical methods to existing data (Andrews et al., 2012). In this way, analysis of existing data should be distinguished from approaches which seek to critically assess the methods or findings of existing research through systematic reviews or meta-analyses (Long-Sutehall et al., 2010). Meta-analyses involve carrying out analysis of one overarching quantitative data set which is comprised of all the available primary data sets within a given area of research. For example, a researcher who carried out a meta-analysis of prevalence rates of violence against women in the last decade would aim to acquire the data from all studies examining the prevalence of violence against women which had been carried out in the last decade. This would result in a data set comprised of all the individual data sets. Analysis of this overarching data set (i.e. meta-analysis) is likely to provide a more accurate assessment of the true prevalence of violence against women over the preceding decade than any one individual data set. This is because its larger sample size would make it less prone to bias and more capable of detecting small effects that might not have been evident in individual data sets. Meta-analyses are discussed in more detail later in this chapter.

Whilst meta-analyses and other analyses of existing quantitative data are relatively common, the same cannot be said for analyses of qualitative data (Hinds et al., 1997; Long-Sutehall et al., 2010), particularly in the social sciences. In other disciplines, for example the arts and humanities, existing data and materials are routinely used to address new research projects and questions. For example, historians will frequently use archives to find existing documents, letters and photographs to examine new questions or objectives. Many traditional data repositories within the arts and humanities hold both quantitative and qualitative data, and there are some existing data services dedicated to qualitative data, for example the 'QUALIDATA' database, which is now part of the UK Data Service in the UK. There has also been an increase in the publication of work which draws on qualitative data obtained through more informal, non-archived sources (Heaton, 2008), though many of these are carried out by one or more of the authors involved in the original research from which the data sets were derived.

Over the last decade, the methodological considerations and practices underpinning analysis of existing qualitative data have gained increasing researcher interest, including special editions of journals (e.g. Barbour and Eley, 2007). However, there remains confusion and controversy over the use of existing qualitative data for additional analysis, with ethical concerns about the re-use of data and consent, the 'problem of data fit,' and the 'problem of not having been there' (see Heaton, 2008, for a review).

Analysis of existing data, whether it concerns quantitative or qualitative data, boasts a number of advantages over the collection and analysis of original data. In addition to being cost-effective and time-saving, analysis of existing data can be particularly useful when the topic is classed as 'sensitive,' and/or participants are 'elusive' or hard to reach (Long-Sutehall et al., 2010). Existing data can be used in the training of researchers and education of students, whilst access to archived data can be particularly beneficial for individuals seeking to develop their research skills and analytical capabilities (Van Den Eynden et al., 2011).

However, there are also disadvantages to working with existing data. Cheng and Phillips (2014) highlight two key issues: missing variables (because the purpose of the original research did not require the collection of some data, or data have been anonymised for confidentiality and variables such as post codes or specific characteristics of participants have been deleted), and familiarity with the data set (new researchers are unaware of the original study-specific nuances, processes and interpretation). Furthermore, there can be specific challenges with using particular types of existing data. For example, data sets collected by the police have a number of methodological weaknesses including inconsistent recording of crimes, missing data and the absence of incidents that were not reported or recorded. Such challenges must be considered when analysing existing data.

Approaches to the analysis of existing data in gender, violence and abuse research

The full range of available sources of existing data is vast and beyond the scope of this chapter. However, there are a number of commonly used existing data sources in research on gender, violence and abuse. These are considered below.

Media and social media

The media is a rich source of existing data. Analysis of media sources has a long history in social research, with such sources often being used as a way of examining attitudes or the 'cultural temperature' of society (Hansen and Machin, 2013). There are two main ways that media reports/sources are used in gender violence research:

1   To provide context or supplementary information to existing research – some research has utilised media reports to provide further detail where there is missing data. A good example of this is Karen Ingala Smith's project, Counting Dead Women (Example 1), which utilises media reports of homicides involving women to provide richer context on the backgrounds and characteristics of these homicides which is not available through other public sources.

2   For addressing new research questions – a common way of using media reports is as a source of existing data for original analysis. In gender, violence and abuse research, recent examples of media analysis include analysis of newspaper/print media reports of domestic violence (Rollè et al., 2014), and femicide-suicide (Richards et al., 2014). Typically, researchers utilising this method will analyse the way the media construct, reflect on or characterise the issue of violence against women, and how the media's approach contributes to a culture of violence towards women (Ardovini-Brooker and Caringella-MacDonald, 2002; Kahlor and Eastin, 2011). Consequently, it is not just the text (and/or images) that is being analysed, but also the processes and understandings of the media (and sometimes the consumer).

Example 1: Karen Ingala Smith's Counting Dead Women project

The Counting Dead Women project, established by Karen Ingala Smith in January 2012, has used media reports of murders of women killed by men to map both the extent of these offences and the links between them. It began as an unofficial project following the murder of a young woman who had been referred to 'nia,' a charity supporting female victims of violence for which Ingala Smith is the chief executive. There was scant information available about how the woman had been killed, so Ingala Smith searched the woman's name online to try and find out more. When carrying out this search she came across numerous reports of other women who had been killed in the previous few days and weeks. Seeing this, Ingala Smith began to keep a database of femicide cases, in which she logged all murders of women and the characteristics of the cases, namely the ages of the women and the accused, the relationship between them and the method and location of the killing. Since January 2012, Ingala Smith has searched 'Google' every day using terms such as: 'woman found dead,' 'woman dead' and 'woman body found.' As the database and project has grown and awareness has increased, members of the public have also helped to collect information by tweeting or emailing news reports directly to Ingala Smith.

Whilst there are obvious limitations to the use of media reports for data collection, including missing information, a lack of control of data quality and biased reporting, the method also has several advantages. First, it provides immediate access to information about cases in real time, as they unfold, and is a quick way of accessing significant amounts of information. Second, it is cost-effective, as the searches are conducted online. Third, it allows for the collection of data at an individual case level. This was particularly beneficial for Ingala Smith's research, as whilst data on homicides can be obtained annually via the Homicide Index, this data is aggregated and reported based on common themes or averages. It therefore does not allow for the scrutiny of specific cases, and provides less detailed information than a media-focused approach.

Ingala Smith's work was used as the basis for the Femicide Census, a database containing information on women killed by men in England and Wales from 2009 to the present day. The Femicide Census was launched in 2015 and produced its first annual report of femicide in 2017. The report detailed all cases of women killed by men in 2016, bringing together the findings from Ingala Smith's Counting Dead Women project and the results of freedom of information requests submitted to police forces in the UK. The acquisition of police data allowed for the verification of the data in the media reports, and ensured that any missing data were included.

Although print media sources, namely newspapers, have been a commonly used source of existing data, other research has utilised non-print media sources such as film (Fernandez-Villanueva et al., 2009), television (Smith, 1999) and even video games (Beck et al., 2012). More recently, with the growth of technology, social media has emerged as an important data source. Although often incorporated within broader categories of media, social media differs from some of the examples listed above. Whereas traditional media is usually made by organisations and consumed by the public, social media is either produced, or co-produced, by members of the public who are also the consumers.

Feminist researchers have used social media analysis to examine online resistance to violence, often labelled digital feminist activism (Horeck, 2014). Adopting a discursive textual analysis, Keller et al. (2016) analysed social media responses to rape culture and experiences of sexual violence by examining posts using the hashtag #BeenRapedNeverReported. Hashtags in the context of social media are words or phrases prefaced with the '#' symbol and employed as a way of connecting one's social media posts with similar posts (by other authors) which use the same hashtag. Keller et al. (2016) combined their discursive textual analysis with interviews with some of the people who used this hashtag on 'Twitter.' Through this process, the researchers were able to explore the context and motivations underpinning the individuals' utilisation of social media activism.

Online forums and discussion boards

Online forums and discussion boards are another popular source of secondary data. Similar to social media, one of the interesting aspects of online forums and discussion boards is that they rely predominantly on members to both generate and consume content (Malinen, 2015). Analysis of forum content is typically approached using either ethnography or content/thematic analysis. In the ethnographic approach, the researcher observes the conversations and interactions between forum users, whilst in the content/thematic analytical approach the researcher identifies specific words or themes within threads (conversations), individual messages or a specified sample of messages. In either case, the researcher can either be covert (analysing the material without declaring their presence) or overt (making users aware they are there).

Westmarland and Graham (2010) analysed online forum discussions to explore viewer reactions to a 2007 BBC TV show which brought together 12 celebrities to form a jury in a fictional rape case. The website accompanying the TV programme linked to a discussion forum where viewers were encouraged to 'post' their 'point of view' on the show and discuss it with other viewers. Westmarland and Graham (2010) examined the 1,588 threads (new discussions) to explore how rape myths were produced and challenged. This methodological approach has also been used to study the online harassment of women, including the harassment of feminist researchers who receive online abuse because of their work (see Vera-Gray, 2017).

Analysing existing documents and official sources of data

Official documents can be a useful source of existing data. There are a number of official sources of data that are useful in gender, violence and abuse research:

1   The Crime Survey for England and Wales (CSEW) – this national victimisation survey collects data on domestic violence, sexual violence and stalking,

and is published by the Office for National Statistics (ONS) (see Chapter 6 for an overview of this survey). The findings of the survey are published annually, and supplementary data files are made available which allow for limited analysis of the data. The data are not re-produced in raw format, but rather are provided in spreadsheets organised around specific demographics. This does not always allow for analysis of different variables together; for example, the CSEW reports on various forms of interpersonal violence by age of victim, gender of victim and relationship to suspect, but these are provided separately in different spreadsheets which do not specify which victim belongs to which category. As a result, a more comprehensive analysis which takes all three variables into account cannot be carried out.

2   Police recorded data – data on some forms of violence and abuse, for example sexual offences, reported to and recorded by the police is usually published alongside the CSEW data in the annual ONS report. Only limited data files are provided, however, which reduces opportunities for analysis. However, other ways of accessing police data are available; agreements can be made between the police and academic researchers or other organisations (the N8 Policing Research Partnership, for example, acts as an enabler for data sharing requests across the North of England), and researchers can submit freedom of information (FOI) requests to public bodies. Example 2 discusses Bows' use of FOI requests in her doctoral research into the rape of older people in the UK.

3   Law transcripts and law reports – these documents, which provide a case analysis including judgements, can provide useful sources of existing data for original analysis. In England and Wales, judgements, transcripts and law reports are available via databases including 'Lexis Nexis' and 'Westlaw.' These reports are usually limited to cases that have set precedents (cases in which a legal decision is recorded for use in future cases), and to appeal cases (Court of Appeal), although not all cases in this latter court are formally reported. Law reports are also published by the Incorporated Council of Law Reporting for England and Wales (ICLR). In addition, it is possible to request transcripts of other more general cases heard in the crown courts via HM Courts and Tribunal Service, although there is usually a cost associated with these. Cases are often reported by other organisations, including the media (e.g. 'The Times' newspaper) and law journals (e.g. 'Criminal Law Review') although these are not checked for accuracy to the same extent as the law reports published by ICLR. One of the authors (Westmarland) used law reports in her doctoral research to examine how rape victims and defendants use human rights in relation to the prosecution process (see Example 3).

4   Homicide Index – the Homicide Index is a database holding data on all recorded homicide cases in England and Wales. It is a 'living document,'

in that it is constantly updated by the police and other criminal justice agencies. Given the level of personal data captured by the index, it is not available to the general public. However, several researchers have utilised the Homicide Index to explore the characteristics and contexts of different types of homicide, including homicide-suicide (Flynn et al., 2009). Similarly, outside of the UK, researchers often utilise homicide data, for example via the FBI supplementary data on homicides (e.g. Roberts, 2009).

5 Other official sources of data include policy reports, minutes from meetings and inquiry/review documents. For example, in gender, violence and abuse research, domestic homicide review reports are being used to examine the characteristics of homicide victims, perpetrators and incidences; to high-light missed opportunities or failings in statutory services; and to identify lessons learned. In a recent evaluation of domestic homicides, Sharp-Jeffs and Kelly (2016) reviewed 32 domestic homicide reviews to identify and explore common themes and learning emerging from these reviews. Ben-bow et al. (2018) used a combination of freedom of information requests and documentary analysis of domestic homicide reviews involving victims and/or perpetrators over the age of 60 to examine victim, offender and offence characteristics and explore whether 'age' differentiated these cases from other domestic homicides. Dobash and Dobash (2015) conducted the largest murder study in the UK and drew on case files of 866 convicted murders. These case files are held in Prison Headquarters London (for those convicted in England/Wales) and Edinburgh (for those convicted in Scotland). The authors sought to develop a more comprehensive picture of homicides, taking into account the backgrounds of victims and offenders as well as statements from a range of professionals involved in the criminal case and management of the offenders. Their analysis specifically allowed for a focus on homicide of women, which they report in a number of articles and their book 'When Men Murder Women' (Dobash and Dobash, 2015).

The following examples discuss the use of some of these forms of existing data in original research.

Example 2: use of Freedom of Information (FOI) requests in research on the rape of older people in the UK

Bows' doctoral research examined rape and serious sexual assault of people aged 60 and over in the UK. The research consisted of three phases, with the first phase specifically concerned with examining the extent of recorded offences involving an older person. There has been very little research on sexual violence amongst older populations, and until 2017, individuals over the age of 59 were excluded from the CSEW module on interpersonal violence (see Chapter 6). As a result, there is a lack of data on the extent and prevalence of sexual violence victimisation amongst people aged 60 and above. In order to examine the incidence of sexual violence against older people, FOI requests were used as a way of gaining information from police forces across the UK on the number of recorded serious sexual offences (rape/assault by penetration) from 1 January 2009 to 31 December 2013 involving a victim aged 60 or over at the time of the offence. These offences were selected because they are the most legally serious sexual offences and because asking for data on all sexual offences may have made the study too broad and therefore more likely to be refused under the exemptions within the FOI Act (see Bows, 2017). However, this did limit the study to these specific offences only. As well as the number of recorded offences, demographic data relating to the victim, perpetrator and incident was requested.

Although the data gained through FOI requests already exist and have been collected by individual forces during the incident recording process, the data are not publicly available or published in any existing reports or databases. However, FOI requests fall outside the 'traditional dichotomy between primary and secondary research' (Savage and Hyde, 2014, p. 8), and individual researchers differ in their view of whether the data analysis is primary or secondary. The analysis of these data was considered to be an original analysis of existing data, as although the data were already in existence prior to the research, they were not publicly available and the analysis of the data was unique to the particular study.

Whilst internationally legislation and policy governing access to information is not a new development (for an overview see Walby and Larsen, 2012), it is relatively new in the UK. The two pieces of legislation governing access to information in the UK are the Freedom of Information Act 2000 (England, Wales and Northern Ireland) and the Freedom of Information Act 2002 (Scotland). Under these Acts, citizens (including those living outside of the UK) are able to make requests for access to data held by public authorities. Public authorities include a range of organisations and institutions, including government departments, local councils, health service bodies (including the National Health Service), schools, colleges, universities, police forces and associated authorities and the armed forces. Requests must be made in writing, most commonly by email, and the authorities have a 20-working day timeframe within which to respond (or request a time extension). The response should either consist of the requested information or a refusal to provide the information, based on one of the exemptions contained in the Acts. As such, there is a positive obligation on the authority to release the data requested, and that is the starting point of the legislation. However, there are 23 exemptions in total and these can create something of a tangled web for researchers seeking to use the legislation to gain access to data (see Bows, 2017, for reflections on negotiating these exemptions).

It has been argued that social researchers use a relatively narrow range of data collection techniques (Lee, 2005), and the need to find innovative methods has been of increasing importance in social science and related disciplines. Despite the comparably widespread use of FOI in other jurisdictions, social scientists, and criminologists in particular, have rarely utilised FOI requests. With respect to gender, violence and abuse research there are currently only a handful of published studies that have employed FOI requests (e.g. Benbow et al., 2018; Women's Aid, 2016; Bows and Westmarland, 2017; Westmarland et al., 2017). Researchers in other fields who use this approach rarely discuss it in their methodological literature, with a few exceptions mainly emerging from medical and health disciplines (Murray, 2012; Farrukh and Mayberry, 2015; for a review see Fowler et al., 2013). As a result, the process of gathering data via FOI requests can appear somewhat opaque even to those who are interested in using it. Therefore, a description of the process is detailed below.

The FOI request made by Bows consisted of two questionnaires which were sent to all police forces in England, Wales and Northern Ireland. The first asked forces for aggregated totals on the number of offences (under Section 1 and Section 2 of the Sexual Offences Act 2003) that had been recorded between 1 January 2009 and 31 December 2014, broken down by year and offence type. It then asked for the overall number of these offences (by year) which involved a victim aged 60 and over. The second questionnaire asked for specific incident data for each recorded case involving a victim aged 60 and over. The individual incident data requested concerned the gender, age group and ethnicity of the victim and the perpetrator; the relationship between the victim and the perpetrator; the location of the sexual offence (for example the victim's home); whether the offence was linked to any other offence; and whether the offender was a known serial sex offender.

The use of FOI requests in the first phase of this study was particularly beneficial as it helped inform the qualitative interviews which followed in Phases 2 and 3. The approach of combining quantitative and qualitative methods in feminist research has been encouraged by feminists (Oakley, 1999; Shapiro et al., 2003), as it has the potential to give a more powerful voice to women's experiences (Hodgkin, 2008), whilst also increasing the likelihood of researchers understanding what they are studying and strengthening their ability to persuade others of the credibility of the research (Reinharz and Davidman, 1992). Whilst there have been some concerns about the incompatibility of qualitative and quantitative paradigms (Bryman, 2006; Kidder and Fine, 1987), a sequential approach can overcome these issues because the data collection methods involve 'collecting data in an iterative process whereby the data collected in one phase contribute to data collected in the next' (Driscoll et al., 2007, p. 21).

Example 3: human rights in the prosecution of rape

In her doctoral research, Westmarland explored the way human rights were used in rape cases by both victims and defendants in relation to the prosecution process. Whilst previous research had involved interviews with those involved in rape trials (victims, defendants and legal personnel), and/or observations of trials and transcripts, only one previous study at the time had examined appeal cases (Cook, 2002). Law reports at appeal stage often include lengthy justifications for the judge's reasoning and decisions. This is in stark contrast to decisions made at earlier stages in the criminal justice process (e.g. Crown Court) where both juries and magistrates' decisions are private and their reasoning immune from scrutiny. Westmarland used law reports, rather than other methods such as interviews with 'key players' such as human rights campaign groups and feminist organisations, because they allowed access to cases within and outside of the UK. Other advantages of using law reports as a data source included their accessibility, low cost and ability to provide a large volume of data. However, as Westmarland notes, the disadvantages of using law reports (and arguably many other documents) is that they are static and there is no opportunity to ask for more detail or clarification.

Re-analysing academic data – meta-analysis

Analysis of existing literature is common within the social sciences. This form of analysis is often conducted through systematic literature reviews and, in some cases, aggregated data from existing studies is analysed (meta-analysis). Meta-analyses can be powerful in 'scaling up' the data from individual studies, allowing researchers to run more sophisticated statistical analyses. In their study of the effectiveness of shelter (refuge) interventions, Jonker et al. (2014) combined the data from ten original studies to analyse data from a total of 726 participants who were female victims of intimate partner violence. They found that shelter interventions were significantly more effective in improving mental health outcomes, in decreasing abuse and in improving social outcomes when compared with control interventions. Although the authors warn that their results should be interpreted with caution given the limited number and quality of the studies involved, these findings are undoubtedly greater than the sum of their parts (i.e. the individual research studies).

A larger number of papers were suitable for review in Wincentak et al.'s (2017) meta-analytic review of the prevalence of teen dating violence. They based their meta-analysis on 101 studies of young people aged 13–18, and found that one in five young people had experienced physical teen dating violence and one in ten had experienced sexual violence. This study was useful in that there were previously divergent findings in terms of individual studies and the prevalence rates they reported, making it difficult to easily make sense of the different findings. A secondary aim of the meta-analysis was therefore to find out why there was such diversity in the rates reported by different studies; namely whether sample age, representation of different cultures, economic disadvantage, family structure and the measurement period and tool that was used could account for such variation. Not surprisingly, the researchers found that some of the variability in existing reports was down to the number of participants of each gender, given the different rates of teen dating violence between girls and boys. However, they also found that age, cultural minority status, economic disadvantage and the use of measurement tools that were particularly broad could also explain the differing rates reported. Wincentak et al. concluded,

> Taken together, the findings provide researchers as well as community agencies, educational partners, and frontline workers with important information to consider in their research, prevention, and intervention efforts addressing this pressing public health issue.
>
> (Wincentak et al., 2017, p. 234)

As well as providing useful information to a wide range of stakeholders, meta-analyses can also be useful in assessing the state of knowledge in a given area. For example, both the Jonker et al. (2014) and the Wincentak et al. (2017) studies (in line with other meta-analyses) raise as many if not more questions than they do answers. Whilst they assess statistically what *has* been asked, they often make commentary about what *has not*, for example Jonker et al. comment on the lack of studies on the cost-effectiveness of shelter interventions. In addition, by providing reasons for the inclusion or exclusion of a study in their meta-analyses, and by assessing the quality of the studies that are included, researchers who carry out meta-analyses are able to make recommendations on study design and research methods that would be useful for the field as it moves forwards. For example, Wincentak et al. note the future value of exploring teen dating violence in terms of context, severity and consequences.

Summary

This chapter has described some of the different forms and sources of existing data that gender, violence and abuse researchers may use. The benefits and limitations of using existing data have been considered. Examples of the various sources of existing data that can be used in feminist research have been presented. These include media sources, online forums and discussion boards, police data and law reports. Such sources of data offer opportunities for researchers to address a range of research questions and generate new knowledge using existing data.

References

Andrews, L., Higgins, A., Andrews, M. W. and Lalor, J. G. (2012) Classic grounded theory to analyse secondary data: Reality and reflections, *The Grounded Theory Review*, *11*(1), pp. 12–26.

Ardovini-Brooker, J. and Caringella-MacDonald, S. (2002) Media attributions of blame and sympathy in ten rape cases, *The Justice Professional*, *15*(1), pp. 3–18.

Barbour, S. and Eley, S. (Eds.) (2007) Refereed special section: Reusing qualitative data, *Sociological Research Online*, *12*(3).

Beck, V. S., Boys, S., Rose, C. and Beck, E. (2012) Violence against women in video games: A prequel or sequel to rape myth acceptance?, *Journal of Interpersonal Violence*, *27*(15), pp. 3016–3031.

Benbow, S., Bhattacharyya, S. and Kingston, P. (2018) Older adults and violence: An analysis of domestic homicide reviews in England involving adults over 60 years of age, *Ageing and Society*, Epub ahead of print 11 January 2018. DOI: 10.1017/S0144686X17001386.

Bows, H. (2017) Researching sexual violence against older people: Reflecting on the use of Freedom of Information requests in a feminist study, *Feminist Review*, *115*(1), pp. 30–45.

Bows, H. and Westmarland, N. (2017) Rape of older people in the United Kingdom: Challenging the 'real-rape' stereotype, *British Journal of Criminology*, *57*(1), pp. 1–17.

Bryman, A. (2006) Integrating quantitative and qualitative research: How is it done?, *Qualitative Research*, *6*(1), pp. 97–113.

Cheng, H. G. and Phillips, M. R. (2014) Secondary analysis of existing data: Opportunities and implementation, *Shanghai Arch Psychiatry*, *26*(6), pp. 371–375.

Cook, K. (2002) *Rape, the End of the Story: A Study of Rape Appeal Cases*. Doctoral Thesis, Manchester: Manchester Metropolitan University.

Dobash, R. E. and Dobash, R. P. (2015) *When Men Murder Women*. Oxford: Oxford University Press.

Donovan, C. and Hester, M. (2009) *Comparing Love and Domestic Violence in Heterosexual and Same Sex Relationships, 2005–2006* [data collection]. UK Data Service, Accessed 10 June 2018, SN: 6332, DOI: 10.5255/UKDA-SN-6332-1.

Driscoll, D. L., Appiah-Yeboah, A., Salib, P. and Rupert, D. J. (2007) Merging qualitative and quantitative data in mixed methods research: How to and why not, *Ecological and Environmental Anthropology*, *3*(1), pp. 19–28.

Farrukh, A. and Mayberry, J. F. (2015) Ethnic variations in the provision of biologic therapy for Crohn's disease: A Freedom of Information study, *Medico-Legal Journal*, *83*(2), pp. 104–108.

Fernandez-Villanueva, C., Revilla-Castro, J. C., Dominguez-Bilbao, R., Gimeno-Jimenez, L. and Almagro, A. (2009) Gender differences in the representation of violence on Spanish television: Should women be more violent?, *Sex Roles*, *61*(1-2), pp. 85-100.

Flynn, S., Swinson, N., While, D., Hunt, I. M., Roscoe, A., Rodway, C., Windfuhr, K., Kapur, N., Appleby, L. and Shaw, J. (2009) Homicide followed by suicide: A cross-sectional study, *The Journal of Forensic Psychiatry & Psychology*, *20*(2), pp. 306-321.

Fowler, A. J., Agha, R. A., Camm, C. F. and Littlejohns, P. (2013) The UK Freedom of Information Act (2000) in healthcare research: A systematic review, *BMJ Open*, *3*(11), pp. 1-7.

Hansen, A. and Machin, D. (2013) *Media and Communication Research Methods*. London: Macmillan Education.

Heaton, J. (2008) Secondary analysis of qualitative data: An overview, *Historical Social Research*, *33*(3), pp. 33-45.

Hinds, P. S., Vogel, R. J. and Clarke-Steffen, L. (1997) The possibilities and pitfalls of doing a secondary analysis of a qualitative data set, *Qualitative Health Research*, *7*(3), pp. 408-424.

Hodgkin, S. (2008) Telling it all: A story of women's social capital using a mixed methods approach, *Journal of Mixed Methods Research*, *2*(4), pp. 296-316.

Horeck, T. (2014) #AskThicke: 'Blurred lines,' rape culture, and the feminist hashtag takeover, *Feminist Media Studies*, *14*(6), pp. 1105-1107.

Jonker, I. E., Sijbrandij, M., van Luijtelaar, M. J., Cuijpers, P. and Wolf, J. R. (2014) The effectiveness of interventions during and after residence in women's shelters: A meta-analysis, *European Journal of Public Health*, *25*(1), pp. 15-19.

Kahlor, L. and Eastin, M. S. (2011) Television's role in the culture of violence toward women: A study of television viewing and the cultivation of rape myth acceptance in the United States, *Journal of Broadcasting & Electronic Media*, *55*(2), pp. 215-231.

Keller, J., Mendes, K. and Ringrose, J. (2016) Speaking 'unspeakable things': Documenting digital feminist responses to rape culture, *Journal of Gender Studies*, *27*(1), pp. 22-36.

Kidder, L. H. and Fine, M. (1987) Qualitative and quantitative methods: When stories converge, *New Directions for Program Evaluation*, *1987*(35), pp. 57-75.

Lee, R. M. (2005) The UK Freedom of Information Act and social research, *International Journal of Social Research Methodology*, *8*(1), pp. 1-18.

Long-Sutehall, T., Sque, M. and Addington-Hall, J. (2010) Secondary analysis of qualitative data: A valuable method for exploring sensitive issues with an elusive population?, *Journal of Research in Nursing*, *16*(4), pp. 335-344.

Malinen, S. (2015) Understanding user participation in online communities: A systematic literature review of empirical studies, *Computers in Human Behavior*, *46*, pp. 228-238.

Murray, C. (2012) Sport in care: Using Freedom of Information requests to elicit data about looked after children's involvement in physical activity, *British Journal of Social Work*, *43*(7), pp. 1347-1363.

Oakley, A. (1999) Paradigm wars: Some thoughts on a personal and public trajectory, *International Journal of Social Research Methodology*, *2*(3), pp. 247-254.

Reinharz, S. and Davidman, L. (1992) *Feminist Methods in Social Research*. Oxford: Oxford University Press.

Richards, T. N., Gillespie, L. K. and Smith, M. D. (2014) An examination of the media portrayal of femicide: Suicides: An exploratory frame analysis, *Feminist Criminology*, *9*(1), pp. 24-44.

Roberts, D. W. (2009) Intimate partner homicide: Relationships to alcohol and firearms, *Journal of Contemporary Criminal Justice*, *25*(1), pp. 67-88.

Rollè, L., Abba, S., Fazzino, R., Marino, E. and Brustia, P. (2014) Domestic violence and newspaper: An explorative study, *Procedia: Social & Behavioral Sciences*, *127*, pp. 504-508.

Savage, A. and Hyde, R. (2014) Using Freedom of Information requests to facilitate research, *International Journal of Social Research Methodology*, *17*(3), pp. 303-317.

Shapiro, M., Setterlund, D. and Cragg, C. (2003) Capturing the complexity of women's experiences: A mixed-method approach to studying incontinence in older women, *Affilia*, *18*(1), pp. 21–33.

Sharp-Jeffs, N. and Kelly, L. (2016) *Domestic Homicide Review (DHR) Case Analysis: Report for Standing Together*. London: London Metropolitan University.

Smith, A. M. (1999) *Girls on Film: Analysis of Women's Images in Contemporary American and 'Golden Age' Hollywood Films*. Master's Thesis, Cleveland, OH: Cleveland State University.

Van den Eynden, V., Corti, L., Woollard, M., Bishop, L. and Horton, L. (2011) *Managing and Sharing Data: A Best Practice Guide for Researchers*, 3rd ed. Colchester: UK Data Archive.

Vera-Gray, F. (2017) 'Talk about a cunt with too much idle time': Trolling feminist research, *Feminist Review*, *115*(1), pp. 61–78.

Walby, K. and Larsen, M. (2012) Access to information and freedom of information requests: Neglected means of data production in the social sciences, *Qualitative Inquiry*, *18*(1), pp. 31–42.

Watts, C. and Vyas, S. (2010) *Contested Development?: Intimate Partner Violence and Women's Employment in Urban and Rural Tanzania* [data catalogue]. UK Data Service, Accessed 10 June 2018, SN: 850417, DOI: 10.5255/UKDA-SN-850417.

Westmarland, N. and Graham, L. (2010) The promotion and resistance of rape myths in an internet discussion forum, *Journal of Social Criminology*, *1*(2), pp. 80–104.

Westmarland, N., Johnson, K. and McGlynn, C. (2017) Under the radar: The widespread use of 'out of court resolutions' in policing domestic violence and abuse in the United Kingdom, *British Journal Of Criminology*, *58*(1), pp. 1–16.

Wincentak, K., Connolly, J. and Card, N. (2017) Teen dating violence: A meta-analytic review of prevalence rates, *Psychology of Violence*, *7*(2), pp. 224–241.

Women's Aid (2016) *Femicide Census: Profiles of Women Killed by Men*. London: Women's Aid.

9 Ethnography

Whilst ethnography is a widely used methodology across social research disciplines, it is perhaps most commonly associated with anthropological research. This chapter provides an overview of the use of ethnography in research examining gender-based violence across criminology, sociology, social policy and health, as well as anthropology and associated disciplines. The chapter opens with a brief introduction to ethnography as an umbrella methodology which incorporates a range of methods, and provides a contextual history of the emergence of ethnography as a methodology in gender and violence research. The chapter then outlines the use of ethnography in feminist research, drawing on examples of how it has been used to research violence and abuse, before discussing the use of ethnography in feminist activism.

Overview of ethnography as a research methodology

Ethnography is a qualitative research methodology concerned with describing people, cultures and behaviours. '"Ethnos" means people, race or cultural group and "graphe" means writing; thus, ethnography literally means writing culture' (Draper, 2015, p. 36). Ethnography can mean different things to different researchers and disciplines. Hammersley and Atkinson (2007) advocate a liberal interpretation of the term, suggesting that ethnography involves the researcher participating, either overly or covertly, in people's daily lives over an extended period of time. This typically involves watching or observing what is happening, listening to what is said, and asking questions/engaging in dialogue with the individuals or groups who are participating in the research. Traditionally, this has involved being physically present in the field; however, technological developments have opened new ways of conducting ethnographic research. This includes the observation of online communities, termed virtual ethnography or 'netnography.' To date, netnography has predominantly been used in media and marketing research, and is defined by Kozinets (2010, p. 60) as 'mediated communications as a source of data to arrive at the ethnographic understanding and representation of a cultural or communal phenomenon.' The method has been identified as particularly suited to the study of topics deemed 'sensitive' (Langer and Beckman, 2005).

There is also no single way of doing ethnography. Skeggs (2007) notes that ethnography is continually transformed through its intersections with other disciplines. It is argued by Skeggs that feminism and ethnography are particularly compatible, as they

> both have experience, participants, definitions, meanings and sometimes subjectivity as a focus and they do not lose sight of context. Just like any feminist research, the ethnographer maps out the physical, cultural and economic possibilities for social action and meaning.
>
> (Skeggs, 2007, p. 426)

Ethnographic work on gender relations was conducted as early as the 1940s by Margaret Mead (O'Reilly, 2008), however it was not until the 1970s that a specifically feminist ethnography emerged (Davis and Craven, 2016). It was during this time, at the height of the second wave women's movement, that feminist research and methods gained more prominence, with feminist ethnography being no exception (Pillow and Mayo, 2012). In this time, it has been used effectively to provide important information about women's lives (Skeggs, 2007). As Stacey (1988) notes, ethnographic methods are ideally suited to feminist research, given the focus on reciprocal relationships between the 'knower' (researcher) and the 'known' (participant). McDowell (2016) suggests that many feminist scholars share the view that ethnography is particularly appropriate to feminist research, as it emphasises the experiential and provides greater respect for research subjects/participants who, some feminists propose, can and should become full collaborators in feminist research. Although feminists engage with a number of ethnographic methods in their research, Davis and Craven (2016) suggest that participant observation is the most common method employed (often in combination with other methods such as oral history interviews).

Conducting ethnography as a woman: embodied researchers

Several female ethnographers have highlighted and reflected on the role of the embodied researcher in qualitative research (Roberts and Sanders, 2005). Whilst many researchers may seek to take an objective perspective, their research is necessarily influenced by multiple factors including the research-er's biases, perspective and skills. These factors, amongst others, contribute to the researcher's 'positionality.' The 'reflexive turn' in qualitative research has emphasised the important of how research positionality affects and shapes data collection and analysis, especially within qualitative inquiry. In ethno-graphic research, the experiences of the researcher themselves, as recorded in field notes and/or research diaries, can form part of the data that is examined. Indeed, it has been argued that individuals gain more insight and understand-ing of other cultures or phenomena through their embodied experiences (Hard-ing, 1991; Davies, 1999). Despite the importance of this approach, it has been argued that researchers are encouraged to edit out gender and sexuality in fieldwork discussions and publications, something which Hanson and Richards (2017) suggest contributes to 'a disembodied presentation of research' (Hanson and Richards, 2017, p. 3). Where it does occur, the inclusion of personal experi-ences in ethnographic work is a gendered process; few male ethnographers disclose their personal experiences, with disclosures tending to occur only in extreme circumstances such as arrests (Perrone, 2010).

Perrone argues that female researchers have a 'unique position investigat-ing cultures in sexually charged field sites' such as licenced venues or other leisure spaces (Perrone, 2010, p. 718). Perrone describes a range of challenges faced by female researchers, including obtaining respect from male research subjects and experiencing harassment and sexual advances. In particular, she notes that female researchers can often experience heightened levels of con-cern and fear of rape or sexual assault. Consequently, Perrone argues, female researchers are often advised to tailor or modify their behaviour, for example by dressing in a manner that will 'diminish their sexuality' or by wearing a ring on their wedding finger to signal that they are 'not available' (see also Chap-ter 5 on interviewing). Whilst risk or fear of violence is not limited to female researchers (see Baird (2017) for example for an account of conducting ethno-graphic research with male gang members as a male researcher), the nature and extent of the (actual and perceived) risk is almost certainly greater for female researchers than for their male counterparts.

Whilst many female researchers experience sexual objectification and harass-ment during fieldwork, there is a lack of literature describing these experiences, as well as a lack of discussion of the dynamics of conducting research in sexu-alised environments (Perrone, 2010; Hanson and Richards, 2017). Where such incidents do occur, they are often left out of ethnographers' 'tales from the field,' contributing to a culture in which the broader environment for female ethnog-raphers is rarely discussed. Perrone (2010) argues that this absence leaves new ethnographers ill-prepared for the practical issues which confront female eth-nographers, although some female ethnographers have published reflections on their experiences (including Perrone) and proposed tips and strategies to prevent, and respond, to harassment in the field (Hanson and Richards, 2017). However, whilst such practical tips may be useful, they have been criticised for accepting sexual harassment in the field as an inevitable consequence of a patriarchal society. According to Hanson and Richards (2017, p. 2), 'This conversation structures sexual assault and violence as problems *women* must learn to deal with if they are to conduct research in social settings structured by patriarchy.'

The extent and degree to which women experience sexual harassment and violence in the field varies. Hanson and Richards (2017) interviewed 56 female ethnographers and found all experienced some form of sexual harassment, objectification and/or assault. There is a depressing irony to gender, violence and abuse researchers experiencing sexual harassment and abuse as part of their research. This irony is particularly acute when those engaging in harassment are representatives of the criminal justice system. Stanko (1998) sought to 'make the invisible visible' in writing up her personal experiences of cat calls and sexualised comments throughout her research into the criminal justice system. Nearly all of the harassment experienced as a researcher by one of the authors (Westmarland) took place whilst she was working on a Home Office funded project on prostitution (later published as Hester and Westmarland, 2004). At the time of the fieldwork, she was a young woman (early 20s) and was often mistakenly labelled as a student by the police with which she was working. She witnessed many misogynistic attitudes whilst travelling with the police at night, during which time she shadowed the policing of kerb crawlers and women involved in prostitution. An officer in one area, for example pointed out individual women with comments such as 'I don't know why she's doing this [selling sex] as she's really bonny [attractive].' At times like this it was difficult to know whether to challenge or to stay quiet, and as a new researcher Westmarland stayed quiet. In another city, she found out that the police in one vice team joked about 'running a book' on which officer would 'get to sleep with her.' Although she did not believe this was actually happening, the very verbalising of this as a possibility made her feel uncomfortable. Whilst now, as an experienced researcher, Westmarland would speak out and see this as a form of harassment, as a very inexperienced young researcher this was something she kept to herself, feeling embarrassed about it.

Many factors, including whether a researcher is a survivor of violence or abuse, can impact on how different researchers experience 'the field.' In some cases, there may not be direct sexual harassment, but the situation the researcher finds themselves in can make them feel vulnerable because of intersections between age, gender, class, sexuality, race or ethnicity, religion, or dis/ability. In the above study where Westmarland was engaged in ethnographic work with the police, there was one occasion where she was nearly put in an uncomfortable situation. Westmarland was sat in the back seat of an unmarked police car with two male officers in the front seats. An industrial estate was being patrolled, where a number of complaints had been received from businesses about it being used for kerb crawlers to take women involved in prostitution to once they had been 'picked up.' A car with two people in was identified for further investigation. In it, the man and woman claimed that they were a company director (male) and secretary (female) having an affair and that is why they were having sexual intercourse in a car on an industrial estate. The 'secretary' was a woman known to the police for her involvement in prostitution and she was asked to leave (consistent with this area's approach to target men who bought sex rather than women who sold it). It was decided that the suspect would be taken to the police station for questioning, but as they called into the station on their radios they were told that the cells were all full at the nearest station. They would therefore have to take the suspect to the next station with available cells in a nearby town. This meant that Westmarland was going to have to travel some distance in the back of the car with a suspect who had just been stopped mid-way through sexual intercourse. Luckily the situation was avoided because the suspect grew concerned about his expensive car being left on an industrial estate, so one of the police officers offered to drive it to the police station to which he was being taken. Putting aside the irony of the suspect's concern about being a victim of car crime while under caution for committing a criminal offence, and the police's willingness to engage with this argument, it worked out well for Westmarland who was able to move out of the back seat of the police car into the front.

Perrone (2010) also reflects on her own experience as a petite, heterosexual and unmarried female researcher investigating drug use in sexualised and heterosexist dance club settings. Challenges included balancing the need to be taken seriously as a researcher and avoiding unwanted sexual advances with negotiating the 'need to go native' and appear as part of the dance club culture she was researching. She recalls experiences of being groped and solicited for sexual acts which ultimately shaped her decisions to refrain from attending events and discontinue conversations with some potential participants. She describes how her sexualised and gendered self both 'granted and inhibited' research relationships in these environments.

This next part of this chapter discusses specific examples of ethnographic research which have been conducted in the context of gender, violence and abuse.

Use of an institutional ethnography to understand prosecutors' accounts of sexual assault case rejections

In the US, Frohmann (1991) spent 17 months observing deputy district attorneys in the sexual assault units of two offices on the West Coast. When writing up this research she used pseudonyms to protect the confidentiality of the people and places studied. Throughout the 17 months, Frohmann took extensive field notes, ultimately acquiring data on seven prosecutors' decision-making across more than 300 cases. In addition, she also conducted more formal interviews with the prosecutors and with police officers who handled some of the cases. Such mixed methods are not unusual within ethnographic research.

By using an ethnographic approach, Frohmann was arguably able to gather coverage of more cases than if she had taken an alternative approach. In addition, she was able to capture much more of the 'day to day' workings than if she had relied on interviews or other research methods alone. It is likely that the prosecutors were not as guarded in their (researcher-observed) daily work as they might have been in an interview, for example one prosecutor described a complainant as a 'cluckhead' (person addicted to crack cocaine) and as being 'street worn':

> She is [a] real street-worn woman. She's not leveling with me-visiting a woman with an unknown address on a bus in Center Heights – I don't buy it.
> (prosecutor, in Frohmann, 1991, p. 218)

Through the ethnography, Frohmann manages to gain an understanding of the complexity of decision-making – delving into the 'logic and organization of prosecutors' decisions to reject/accept cases for prosecution' (Frohmann, 1991, p. 224). The data Frohmann presents appears far less sanitised and describes a more complicated and less linear account of decision-making than many of the more modern studies on prosecutors, which have tended to rely more heavily on case file analysis and/or interviews. This may be because policies and procedures have tightened up this decision-making process and/or because the ethnography took place nearly 30 years ago in a different organisational culture. Without doubt, it would be more difficult, and likely impossible, to conduct a similar study in the UK in modern times due to data protection, the sensitivity (and politics) of rape prosecutors' decision-making and the inability for scholars to spend such long periods of time in the field. The length of time included in Frohmann's ethnographic research is important, as it is likely that it was the fact she was there for so long that meant the prosecutors began talking more freely about the cases allowing her to observe their 'usual' working environment more closely.

Use of autoethnography to research street harassment

Some researchers have linked elements of autobiography with ethnography to create autoethnographies. Autoethnography is seen as both a process and a product (Ellis et al., 2011), and is an approach that utilises personal experiences to understand broader socio-cultural experiences. Autoethnography seeks to

make visible the subjective decision-making inherent in research, and to identify how these decisions are linked to personal experience. As Ellis et al. (2011)
explain,

> For instance, a researcher decides who, what, when, where, and how to
> research, decisions necessarily tied to institutional requirements (e.g., Insti-
> tutional Review Boards), resources (e.g., funding), and personal circum-
> stance (e.g., a researcher studying cancer because of personal experience
> with cancer). . . . Consequently, autoethnography is one of the approaches
> that acknowledges and accommodates subjectivity, emotionality, and the
> researcher's influence on research, rather than hiding from these matters or
> assuming they don't exist.
>
> (Ellis et al., 2011, paragraph 3)

Chubin (2014) used autoethnography to illustrate survival from sexual harassment in the streets of Tehran, Iran. She drew on personal experiences of
growing up, of walking with her mother in the streets and witnessing sexual
harassment, of adapting her clothing and behaviour to remain 'honourable' and
of her own experiences of sexual harassment; how she acted, and how she felt
afterwards. Within the paper she reflected on an occasion she spent drinking
with friends after being in a shared taxi with a man who sat too close and took
up too much space. She addressed the fact that as she shared her experiences
of feeling powerless and frustrated by the journey, her friends began to share
similar stories.

> 'What the hell do they think? Why do these assholes let themselves act this
> way?' I again ask the question that is bugging me over these years. 'When I
> once yelled at a guy who was rubbing my thigh in the taxi . . .,' Sahar pauses,
> takes another shot, and tells the rest of the story, 'The driver told me "now
> that you are servicing men with the way you dress, what's wrong with ser-
> vicing them this way." Can you believe he took his side?' We look at each
> other in despair, and nod our heads meaning that we all know a similar story.
> 'Exactly!' Narges tells her story to prove the same point, 'Once my friends
> and I were on a minibus after a school day, and there were a group of work-
> ers on the bus sitting right behind us. They started talking dirty and one of
> them grabbed my boob. I yelled out and as I expected their supervisor to yell
> at them, he just looked at the guys and told them, "didn't I tell you not to do
> this to buzz killers?"' Sahar, Narges and I started laughing out loud at the
> nonsensical, stupid comments of these guys we had carried in our memo-
> ries for years. We almost couldn't believe someone would actually think this
> way. We laughed harder and harder until tears were coming out. We wiped

our tears pretending, even to ourselves, the tears were the result of laughing hard. After several moments of heavy silence I pulled the DVD we had bought that day out of my bag, 'Let's watch a movie!' I suggested to ease the pain I felt was growing inside us. I leaned back on the couch, however, with a smile; I lit my cigarette and enjoyed the almost freeing feeling of exoneration watching the trace of the smoke vanish somewhere around the ceiling. It was as if the iceberg of guilt I had been carrying on my back all these years, freezing my bone marrow, was melting down. 'I knew it was not me,' I thought to myself, 'It really happens to everyone.'

(Chubin, 2014, pp. 188–189)

For Chubin, facing various stereotypes about the oppression she faces as a Muslim woman, it was important to write her story in order to provide a 'window into the lives' of women who are silenced within a patriarchal culture, especially when such experiences feel humiliating and can make the writer feel vulnerable. It is perhaps not surprising then, that Chubin published her autoethnography under a different name to her own in order to protect her identity.

Inside the sexual assault forensic examination room – conducting ethnographic research through the role of a victim advocate

Mulla (2008) spent 42 months working as a victim advocate in an emergency room in the US, observing a total of 44 forensic examinations. She was there in a dual role of trained rape and domestic violence victim advocate and anthropological researcher. The victim-survivors she was supporting were given the choice not to participate in the research and only have her work as their advocate. However, no victim did ask her to exclude their case from her research. She did not ask any additional questions of the victims other than those asked in her advocate role, at the time or afterwards, and only used information that was gathered as part of the advocate support. She explained, 'The rape crisis intervention is so highly structured that I did not feel comfortable imposing another layer of organization or interrogation on the victims' (Mulla, 2008, p. 23). All of the note taking was done after the support had taken place – no recording or writing for research purposes was done in the hospital at the time of the support intervention.

Although she does not explicitly make this claim, one of the key advantages of Mulla's work is that there is a great depth of analysis and the detail of the cases she describes, yet she did not need to rely on the victim's memory at such a traumatic time nor impose additional 'requests' upon them. In many of her examples, it is inconceivable to see how Mulla could have got the subtly of knowledge through any other method. For example, one of the cases she describes is that of 'Keisha.' Keisha was a teenage girl who had been brought into the emergency room after being raped at a party at home. She was brought in by her father – who had just the day before been released from prison for a previous sexual assault on Keisha (in fact the party was to celebrate his release). Mulla provides extensive detail about the nurse examiner's behaviour when working with Keisha and with Keisha's wider family, describing her frustrations with the equipment and her verbal and non-verbal communication. At one point, Mulla describes hearing a loud debate in the waiting room, although Keisha, 'the only silent person in the entire room,' was sitting quietly and not actively engaging in the debate (Mulla, 2008, p. 7). The debate Mulla overheard was about whether or not Keisha should take the morning-after pill, to prevent any potential pregnancy. She describes how this continued:

> When it became clear that she [her mother] would not be allowed in the forensic examination with her daughter, Keisha's mother became very concerned that the nurse would offer her daughter a morning-after pill without consulting her [. . .]
>
> Taking a cue from my training as a patient advocate, I assured her mother that Keisha would not be coerced into taking any medication, and that if Keisha were to accept the morning-after pill, it would most likely not have any permanent disabling effects on her reproductive system. "I heard that stuff can keep you from having babies ever," she frowned. Though she did not insist on being present at the examination, Keisha's mother was adamant that the forensic nurse provide her with further information about the morning-after pill before administering it, a message I passed on to the nurse before the examination started. Kelly was the nurse examiner on-call that morning. As we walked to the examination room and away from her mother, Keisha broke her silence for the second time and initiated a conversation about not wanting to be pregnant or sick.
>
> (Mulla, 2008, p. 8)

After the examination had been completed, Keisha's mother was informed that Keisha had elected to take the morning-after pill and that she had taken the first dose and the second was needed 12 hours later – assuring her that the pill would not result in any permanent damage to her daughter's reproductive system:

> She then handed an envelope containing the pills to Keisha's mother – the time for the second dosage was written on the envelope in thick, black

magic marker. Kelly warned that Keisha may experience nausea and that she should eat something before the second dose: 'If she throws up, you have to call us because then the pills won't work.'

(Mulla, 2008, p. 9)

Mulla reflected on her concerns that the mother, who was worried and reluctant about Keisha being given the morning after pill, was now being placed as the sole carer of Keisha and relied upon to give the second dose of the pill. This concern was more pertinent given that Keisha's mother had seemingly invited her father back into the family home even though he had previously sexually abused Keisha:

> It was only then that I realized the heated conversation I had overheard earlier that morning was around Keisha's mother's reasons for letting the father return to their home. Keisha's grandmothers, aunts, and cousins were upset that he had been allowed into the home given his known history of abuse against his daughter.

(Mulla, 2008, p. 10)

In this case, it became apparent that Keisha's aunt shared Mulla's concerns about the administration of the second dose of the morning after pill, and consequently took down the administration instructions so she could act as a back-up to Keisha's mother. The dynamics of this case took place both inside and outside the examination room, spanned a period of a few hours and manifested themselves in a way that is unlikely to be picked up by a formal interview schedule. It is important that such dynamics are documented and used, where appropriate, to inform practice in forensic medical examinations. This work demonstrates the advantages of using an ethnographic approach to gain an in-depth understanding of gender, violence and abuse.

Ethnography as part of an anthropological approach – Polish women's experiences of domestic violence and engagement with services in Scotland

For her doctoral research, Johnson (2017) conducted an ethnographic study examining Polish women's experiences of violence and service engagement in Scotland. Over an 18-month period she carried out a multi-sited ethnography, focusing on domestic violence, domestic violence service providers and Polish women's engagement with services. Johnson's work was multidisciplinary in nature, but one of its key aims was to contribute an anthropological perspective on domestic violence and service provision. This anthropological perspective on domestic abuse is one that she and others (e.g. Wies and Haldane, 2011) have noted has been missing, especially from European and British anthropology (less so in American anthropology) – with anthropologists preferring to examine violence in the public rather than the private sphere. Hence, she argues that domestic violence has wrongly been overlooked in applied anthropological domains:

> Anthropology is uniquely positioned to study domestic violence, given the holistic, nuanced and intimate understandings that the discipline's ethnographic methods and outputs afford . . . this is particularly acute in the context of critical engagement with service provision.
>
> (Johnson, 2017, pp. 43–44)

For Johnson, it was important to use placements at more than one organisation in order to look at relationships and interactions between individuals, organisations and communities. Throughout the placements, Johnson collected data via participant observation and, wherever suitable, ethnographic interviewing; conducting 'conversations with purpose,' whilst embedded within the research context (Burgess, 2002, p. 102). This included partaking in discussions with staff, attending meetings, reading through case files, helping out with small menial tasks and shadowing workers as they supported and advocated for clients. Common day-to-day tasks involved sitting in on crisis counselling sessions and assisting staff in providing support, for example by making cups of tea, filling out forms, assisting with childcare and sharing useful information where possible. The work also included assisting staff supporting women in refuge accommodation. This involved going out to the refuges every week to check in and provide support if required. As these tasks mostly comprised activities typically delegated to new employees and students as they 'learn the ropes,' Johnson found that the presence and actions of the researcher did not appear markedly unusual or invasive within the research setting.

As with the previous example (Mulla, 2008), Johnson worked as both a member of staff and a researcher. As a result, she had to be flexible in her implementation of pre-determined ethical best practice, adapting her decisions appropriately as the fieldwork progressed:

> Before starting my fieldwork, I had prepared letters of consent for each research participant to sign, but staff members felt this approach was too cumbersome and invasive for the day-to-day operations of the services. While respecting this, I made it clear to the women I met that I was happy to talk more about my research or how their information would be used, and

offered a card with my contact details on, in case they had any further questions. . . . Almost all of the women agreed to my observing their interactions – even women who were nervous about accessing the service for the first time, or who appeared to be in periods of heightened trauma or crisis. I suspect that some women heard the word 'student' and agreed to my presence, just keen to progress with the meeting, however others said they felt it was important I understand their experiences, and wanted to contribute to knowledge brought about by domestic violence research.

(Johnson, 2017, p. 55)

Following Simpson (2011), Johnson viewed ethical conduct as 'processual' – as something that evolved as new dilemmas emerged. She describes her ethics as being 'embedded in praxis' (Johnson, 2017, p. 70) – requiring an ongoing negotiation with her research participants, partner organisations and supervisors.

Summary

This chapter has provided an overview of the use of ethnographic methods in feminist research. Overlapping with Chapter 3 on ethics, there are particular considerations that need to be taken into account when carrying out ethnographic research. These considerations are explored within the first part of this chapter and within some of the examples (particularly that of Johnson). Several of the examples also depict some form of dual role for the researcher, an approach which requires particular care within ethnographic research. One of the underlying arguments of this chapter is that, despite the challenges associated with ethnographic methods, an ethnographic approach provides a breadth of information and depth of analysis rarely associated with other research methods. Therefore, whilst they can be time consuming and can require continuous focus on ethical practice, ethnographic methods represent an invaluable resource which should be considered by researchers who study gender, violence and abuse.

References

Baird, A. (2017) Dancing with danger: Ethnographic safety, male bravado and gang research in Colombia, *Qualitative Research*, *18*(3), pp. 342–360.
Burgess, R. G. (2002) *In the Field: An Introduction to Field Research*. Abingdon: Routledge.
Chubin, F. (2014) You may smother my voice, but you will hear my silence: An autoethnography on street sexual harassment, the discourse of shame and women's resistance in Iran, *Sexualities*, *17*(1/2), pp. 176–193.

Davies, C. A. (1999) *Reflexive Ethnography: A Guide to Researching Selves and Others*. London: Routledge.

Davis, D. and Craven, C. (2016) *Feminist Ethnography: Thinking through Methodologies, Challenges and Possibilities*. Lanham, MD: Rowman & Littlefield.

Draper, J. (2015) Ethnography: Principles, practice and potential, *Nursing Standard*, *29*(36), pp. 36–41.

Ellis, C., Adams, T. E. and Bochner, A. P. (2011) Autoethnography: An overview, *Forum: Qualitative Social Research*, *12*(1), Art. 10.

Frohmann, L. (1991) Discrediting victims' allegations of sexual assault: Prosecutorial accounts of case rejections, *Social Problems*, *38*(2), pp. 213–226.

Hammersley, M. and Atkinson, P. (2007) *Ethnography: Principles in Practice*, 3rd ed. London: Routledge.

Hanson, R. and Richards, P. (2017) Sexual harassment and the construction of ethnographic knowledge, *Sociological Forum*, *32*(3), pp. 587–609.

Harding, S. (1991) *Whose Science? Whose Knowledge?: Thinking from Women's Lives*. Ithaca, NY: Cornell University Press.

Hester, M. and Westmarland, N. (2004) *Tackling Street Prostitution: Towards an Holistic Approach*. London: Home Office.

Johnson, K. (2017) *Domestic Violence, Liminality and Precarity in the British Borderlands-Polish Women's Experiences of Abuse and Service Engagement in Edinburgh*. Doctoral Thesis, Durham: Durham University.

Kozinets, R. V. (2010) *Netnography*. London: Sage.

Langer, R. and Beckman, S. C. (2005) Sensitive research topics: Netnography revisited, *Qualitative Market Research: An International Journal*, *8*(2), pp. 189–203.

McDowell, L. (2016) Doing gender: Feminism, feminists and research methods in human geography, In: L. McDowell and J. Sharp (Eds.) *Space, Gender, Knowledge: Feminist Readings* (pp. 105–114). London: Routledge.

Mulla, S. A. (2008) There is no place like home: The body as the scene of the crime in sexual assault intervention, *Home Cultures*, *5*(3), pp. 301–325.

O'Reilly, K. (2008) *Key Concepts in Ethnography*. London: Sage.

Perrone, D. (2010) Gender and sexuality in the field: A female ethnographer's experience researching drug use in dance clubs, *Substance Use and Misuse*, *45*(5), pp. 717–735.

Pillow, W. and Mayo, C. (2012) Feminist ethnography: Histories, challenges and possibilities, In: S. N. Hesse-Biber (Ed.) *Handbook of Feminist Research: Theory and Praxis*, 2nd ed. (pp. 187–205). London: Sage.

Roberts, M. and Sanders, T. (2005) Before, during and after: Realism, reflexivity and ethnography, *The Sociological Review*, *53*(2), pp. 294–313.

Simpson, B. (2011) Ethical moments: Future directions for ethical review and ethnography, *Journal of the Royal Anthropological Institute*, *17*(2), pp. 377–393.

Skeggs, B. (2007) Feminist ethnography, In: P. Atkinson, S. Dalmont, A. Coffey, J. Lofland and L. Lofland (Eds.) *Handbook of Ethnography* (pp. 426–442). London: Sage.

Stacey, J. (1988) Can there be a feminist ethnography?, *Women's Studies International Forum*, *11*(1), pp. 21–27.

Stanko, E. A. (1998) Making the invisible visible in criminology: A personal journey, In: S. Holdaway and P. Rock (Eds.) *Thinking about Criminology* (pp. 35–54). London: UCL Press.

Wies, J. R. and Haldane, H. J. (2011) Ethnographic notes from the front lines, In: J. R. Wies and H. J. Haldane (Eds.) *Anthropology at the Front Lines of Gender-Based Violence* (pp. 1–18). Nashville, TN: Vanderbilt University Press.

PART III

Research praxis - using feminist research

10 Influencing and being influenced by activism

Understanding the relationship between feminist research and activism is important both in terms of how research on gender, violence and abuse developed originally but also how it maintains its relevance moving forward. Ackerly and True (2010) note that feminist research is indebted to the women's movements of the 1960s and 70s, with many of the early consciousness raising groups leading to 'personal issues' such as marital rape, women's health, employment discrimination and sexual harassment becoming key political concerns and demands. Consciousness raising as a method, they highlight, successfully revalued personal experiences and feelings as interlinked with politics and society. In fact, the development of women's studies as a sub-discipline (usually but not exclusively of Sociology) came out of such concerns and demands. Burghardt and Colbeck (2005) describe Women's Studies as being *'built by pioneering scholars who dedicated themselves to claiming space in the curriculum for women's diverse experiences and societal contributions'* (p. 301). In the USA, 300 women's studies units are said to have been opened in the 1970s, and by the mid-1990s this figure was thought to be over 700 (National Women's Studies Association, 1995, cited in Burghardt and Colbeck, 2005). Equivalent figures are not available for the UK, but a similar pattern of growth (though not on the same scale) was followed. Whereas the US opened standalone women's studies units/departments, women's studies in the UK more often took the form of degree programmes or modules which ran within existing social sciences departments such as sociology, social policy and/or social work. Sadly, such programmes have been in steady decline over recent years (for example Westmarland was the last ever student to graduate with a women's studies qualification (with Psychology) from Teesside University, her undergraduate University – though the Centre for Women's Studies at the University of York, where she studied for her MA Women's Studies, is still going strong).

Just as feminist activism has given rise to feminist research, feminist research can in turn influence feminist activism. Indeed, research is often a fundamental component of social change movements (Choudry, 2013). Some research methods are particularly well suited to sit alongside activist agendas. Bell (2015) argues that feminist activist ethnography is an especially useful method of activist research, as it is not only relevant to gender-related research but also has broader relevance as a form of resistance to neoliberalist injustices more generally (for example, her own research focuses on environmental injustices). Similarly, some arts-based research methods, because of their strong links to participatory action research, often have an easy affinity with activism. However, this is not to preclude other forms of research methods being used by activists or in an activist setting. Indeed, it has been argued that it is the questions that are asked and the purpose of the analysis which are greater indicators than methods as to what constitutes activist research (Naples, 1998).

Activist research within the academy

One of us (Westmarland) has many years of personal experience of being an 'academic activist.' This is a term used by those who wish to distinguish themselves from being 'blue skies,' 'ivory tower' scholars, and who are upfront about not only wanting to see change in society in connection with their area of research, but also working actively towards making that change happen. Although the label of 'academic activist' is a recent one, there is nothing new about activist scholarship, which dates back at least as far as Aristotle (Calhoun, 2008). For Westmarland, being an academic activist means being willing to take on voluntary positions within women's sector non-governmental organisations, joining in feminist campaigns and marches, being an activist on an organised community/political and a personal level and being involved in the 'grassroots' work of the feminist women's liberation movement. It means action not silence, and deeds not words. It also means being creative within the academy, and using the privilege that comes with an academic post to best use. Indeed, Westmarland considers her greatest education to have come from her activist sisters within the violence against women sector, particularly from the Rape Crisis movement.

In India, academic feminists who fuse activism with academic theory often use the term 'organic intellectuals' – refusing to be separated from grassroots calls for action (Grewal, 2008, p. 161). This was developed from Gramsci (1971), who differentiated between 'traditional' intellectuals (scholars who see themselves as detached from society) and 'organic' intellectuals (the thinkers and organisers from any social class). Other, similar terms to 'academic activist' are 'public criminologist' or 'public sociologist.' These terms are used to indicate that an academic is engaged with 'the public' in their research, but are less suggestive of the more political, social movement-based actions that the term 'activist' brings with it. Hale (2008) points out that most students are asked to 'leave their politics at the door' when entering graduate training programmes, yet in fact we find politics in academia at 'every turn.'

That academics would want to conduct research that has the potential to create change, be it at an individual or societal level, might sound obvious to some. But this is not a given. There is an ongoing backlash within academia against the idea that a core part of being an academic should be creating 'real world' change, with many live debates concerning this issue. This is also a situation that has changed over time. Twenty years ago, the idea that research impact would be so core to the work of so many academics would not have been predicted by many in the field. The practice of incentivising research impact through the Research Excellence Framework (REF), which allocates financial and other rewards to those universities who can demonstrate the most far-reaching research impact, has probably made the greatest difference. Other 'nudges' towards the importance of research impact are its inclusion in application forms for UK Research Council funding. This is discussed further in Chapter 11. The purpose here is not to make an argument that those involved in creating and documenting the impact of their research are therefore by definition academic activists. Rather, it is to demonstrate that academic activists (including Westmarland) have been made to feel more welcome and more central to academic life than in previous years.

The next part of this chapter moves on to consider two examples of the fusion of academic feminist theory and grassroots activism – the first on research and activism on the topic of sexual violence in UK higher education, and the second on the work of a feminist research centre in India called the Centre for Women's Studies and Development.

Example: sexual violence in higher education

Sexual violence in higher education is one area where there has been a particularly strong link between activism and research in many areas of the world. On the one hand, simply teaching about a topic such as sexual violence within the academy can be a form of activism in itself. It means actively engaging with the knowledge that there are victim-survivors and also perpetrators both within our student groups and amongst our academic colleagues. It means being prepared to see and name what is around us in our everyday lives. Often, in teaching gender, violence and abuse, lecturers will be seen as an 'expert' that a student can go to for advice and/or a safe person to which to make a disclosure.

New lecturers and their managers should therefore be aware that there is a definite additional workload associated with teaching gender, violence and abuse. This is on top of the general additionality that operating in a feminist manner within higher education brings with it. At an administrative level, this can result in the additional workload associated with being seen as the 'diversity' 'person' [sic], or the departmental lead for Athena SWAN (Scientific Women's Academic Network), a UK scheme which seeks to recognise gender equality in higher education. Administrative roles aside, challenging sexism (and racism) within the academy is time consuming, sometimes all encompassing, but essential. As stated by Ahmed,

> To be a feminist at work is or should be about how we challenge ordinary and everyday sexism, including academic sexism. This is not optional: it is what makes feminism feminist.
>
> (Ahmed, 2017, p. 14)

Whilst teaching in itself can be a form of activism, there are also additional ways in which scholars become activists and activists become scholars. Many individuals hold overlapping positions, including those who have sought to make a difference in terms of the politics of gender, violence and abuse in higher education. This has been particularly apparent in terms of sexual violence and harassment.

Sara Ahmed is one feminist scholar who has taken a particularly bold and high-profile stance in the UK, resigning from her position at Goldsmiths College, London, in protest of their response (or lack of) to sexual harassment. Her 2017 book, 'Living a Feminist Life,' was written partly while still employed in the academy and partly following her resignation as Professor of race and cultural studies. At the time, in May 2016, Ahmed resigned publicly – announcing it on her public blog feministkilljoys.com, explicitly linking her resignation to the failure of her institution to respond appropriately to sexual harassment and stating that 'resignation is a feminist issue.' She wrote,

> I have resigned in protest against the failure to address the problem of sexual harassment. I have resigned because the costs of doing this work have been too high.
>
> (Ahmed, 2016, *Resignation is a feminist issue*, feministkilljoys blog)

The level of activism in the UK on the area of sexual harassment in higher education has increased exponentially over the last three years (though it has been active elsewhere for far longer). An example of this is the emergence of the '1752 Group' (see www.1752group.com). As a group of feminist academics, they focus on both academic research and activism, describing themselves as 'a UK-based research and lobby organization working to end sexual misconduct in higher education' ('About Us' page, www.1752group.com).

In a different type of resistance which itself was inspired by Ahmed's work on diversity and complaining as feminist work, Downes publicly resisted the showing of a film at the university where she worked. The film was about prison and criminal justice reform, and had positive reviews, but was created by a convicted perpetrator of domestic violence against a student. Following a number of complaints and debates about whether the film should still be shown once the creator's identity was known, the decision was made to go ahead with its screening. Downes concluded,

> However, allowing the screening to proceed unchallenged leaves me complicit in allowing Salter to continue to have his work accessed and validated in academic spaces. Doing nothing therefore contributes to the institutional silencing of sexual misconduct and abuse of power. Allowing silence to spread outwards throughout Higher Education spaces across the country.
> (Downes, 2018, Harm and Evidence Research
> Collaborative (HERC), www.oucriminology.wordpress.com)

Drawing on her work with McGlynn and Westmarland on the importance of recognition for survivors – the 'significance of the experience being acknowledged' (McGlynn et al., 2017, p. 182) – she wrote,

> The power of recognition is threaded through every interaction a survivor has around them. With friends and family, on social media, in workplaces and yes, in Higher Education institutions and other spaces of learning. Judith Herman taught us that an abuser demands nothing from the wider community. To look away, ignore it, just watch the film and stop complaining. This can be much easier to hear, as Herman described "it is very tempting to take the side of the perpetrator. All the perpetrator asks is that the bystander do nothing" (Herman, 1992, p. 7). Public recognition in community is crucial for survivors.
> (Downes, 2018, Harm and Evidence Research
> Collaborative (HERC), www.oucriminology.wordpress.com)

In different ways, Ahmed, the 1752 group and Downes have all been willing to not only academically theorise the problem of sexual violence in higher education, but also act on an individual, personal basis in an effort to raise awareness, reframe the way the issue is seen, seek to create change and demonstrate to survivors that 'the institution' is made up of a variety of different voices – including feminist voices.

Example: Centre for Women's Studies and Development, Panjab University, India

Grewal's (2008) article on feminist academics in Indian Punjabi society is aptly entitled 'Theorising Activism, Activizing Theory.' Here, she describes the ways in which the Centre for Women's Studies and Development (CWSD) developed, the challenges it faced and how it serves as a challenge to what she calls the *'academy-centered interpretation of feminism'* (pg. 161), whereby

> attention solely to theorizing feminism reinforces the privilege still existing in the wealthy, sanitized, and dissociated model present among may university professionals of the West.
>
> (p. 161)

In contrast, she describes how the CWSD serves to fuse activism with theory, operating at different levels from the grassroots to institutions to structures. Faculty at the SWSD seek to bring into clearer focus the conditions of women and girls in the region in which they are based, specifically

> To force the hand of patriarchy so that the girl-children and women in the northern states of Punjab, Haryana, and Himachal Pradesh have a fair chance a) to live and b) to live with dignity.
>
> (p. 165)

Activism, and the creation of 'real world' change, is therefore at the core of members of the CWSD work. It goes beyond this though, and Grewal describes how the CWSD hopes to show a different way forward, a more integrated approach for feminist academics to follow, and one that nuances what it means to be a feminist academic. They hope to create a new way of working which does not privilege European-American academic models or even dismantles them – ultimately using feminist methodologies, critiques and activism which can redefine the very purpose of the academy in postcolonial societies.

The CWSD way of what it means to be a feminist academic and the embeddedness of theory and activism, is one that now sounds 'on trend' with the rise of Western understandings around the need for research impact and more nuanced understandings of feminist methodologies alongside the rejection of the possibility of so called 'objective' knowledge. But when the CWDS was established, in 1980, this was a far more radical way of being a feminist within the academy. From its origins as a response to the realisation that there had been a deterioration of the economic, social and political status of women amidst a backdrop of seemingly progressive policies, the CWDS continues to focus their work on the issues that affect women in Indian society:

> Our vision is to produce creative, theoretically informed and empirically rich research that will help establish women and gender issues as critical, indispensable components of every aspect of education, development and state policy.
>
> (CWDS website, About us, www.cwds.ac.in/about-us/history-2/)

As well as their pioneering research agenda, they also run postgraduate programmes on women and gender studies, short courses and conferences, ensuring new generations of feminist scholars are trained and can spread the CWDS learning.

Summary

This chapter has given a short flavour of some of the ways in which academics are influenced by activism and vice versa. It has described how the increasing overlaps have been able to become more visible and valued in the West – a different way of doing academic feminism – but one that has already been successfully modelled elsewhere, for example through the long-standing work of the Centre for Women's Development Studies (CWDS) in India. As Director (Westmarland) and Deputy Director (Bows) of the Durham University Centre for Violence and Abuse (CRiVA), which has research impact, strong partnerships with those outside of the academy and social change at its heart, we are grateful to our sisters in other parts of the world from which we can learn. Here in the UK we have lagged behind in addressing a problem quite literally on our academic doorsteps – the issue of sexual violence at university. This lag might in part be due to academics feeling previously as though they need to keep their 'academic' work and their 'activism' separate, and not be seen to be too 'troublesome' and challenging at work. Of feeling that within the academy, the personal must never become the political or the intellectual. The impact agenda has lessened this to some extent, although it remains difficult for those on precarious contracts to raise challenges and complain. Ultimately though, some will leave the academy, resigning privately or publicly as Ahmed did, unable to reconcile the realities of negotiating patriarchal academies with 'Living a Feminist Life' (the title of Ahmed's subsequent book).

References

Ackerly, B. and True, J. (2010) Back to the future: Feminist theory, activism, and doing feminist research in an age of globalization, *Women's Studies International Forum*, *33*(5), pp. 464–472.

Ahmed, S. (2016) Resignation is a feminist issue, *Feministkilljoys Blog*, 27 August. Available at: www.feministkilljoys.com/2016/08/27/resignation-is-a-feminist-issue/ (Accessed: 28 June 2018).

Ahmed, S. (2017) *Living a Feminist Life*. Durham, NC: Duke University Press.

Bell, S. E. (2015) Bridging activism and the academy: Exposing environmental injustices through the feminist ethnographic method of photovoice, *Human Ecology Review*, *21*(1), pp. 27–58.

Burghardt, D. A. and Colbeck, C. L. (2005) Women's studies faculty at the intersection of institutional power and feminist values, *Journal of Higher Education*, *76*(3), pp. 301–330.

Calhoun, C. (2008) Foreword, In: C. R. Hale (Ed.) *Engaging Contradictions: Theory, Politics, and Methods of Activist Scholarship* (pp. xiii–xxv). Berkeley, CA: University of California Press.

Choudry, A. (2013) Activist research practice: Exploring research and knowledge production for social action, *Socialist Studies*, *9*(1), pp. 128–151.

Downes, J. (2018) The injustice of injustice: Making a feminist complaint and resisting abuses of power within Higher Education institutions, *Harm & Evidence Research Collaborative (HERC) Blog*, 22 May. Available at: www.oucriminology.wordpress.com/2018/05/22/the-injustice-of-injustice-making-a-feminist-complaint-and-resisting-abuses-of-power-within-higher-education-institutions/ (Accessed: 28 June 2018).

Gramsci, A. (1971) *Selections from the Prison Notebooks*. New York, NY: International Publishers.

Grewal, J. (2008) Theorizing activism, activizing theory: Feminist academics in Indian Punjabi society, *NWSA Journal*, *20*(1), pp. 161–183.

Hale, C.R. (2008) Introduction, In: C.R. Hale (Ed.) *Engaging Contradictions: Theory, Politics, and Methods of Activist Scholarship* (pp. 1–28). California: University of California Press.

Herman, J. L. (1992) *Trauma and Recovery: The Aftermath of Violence: From Domestic Abuse to Political Terror*. New York, NY: Basic Books.

McGlynn, C., Downes, J. and Westmarland, N. (2017) Seeking justice for survivors of sexual violence: Recognition, voice and consequences, In: E. Zinsstag and M. Keenan (Eds.) *Restorative Responses to Sexual Violence: Legal, Social and Therapeutic* (pp. 179–191). Abingdon: Routledge.

Naples, N. (1998) Women's community activism and feminist activist research, In: N. Naples (Ed.) *Community Activism and Feminist Politics: Organizing across Race, Class and Gender* (pp. 1–27). London: Routledge.

11 Using research to influence policy and practice

The importance of research 'impact,' for example influencing or shaping policy and practice, is an increasing requirement for social research internationally. The concept of impact within research is much broader than the dissemination of findings at the end of a study. Rather, the majority of research funding bodies now requires research to have 'real world' impact built into research plans from the start of the project.

This chapter explains the ways in which gender, violence and abuse research can be used to influence (and hopefully improve) policy and practice. The chapter examines research that was carried out in conjunction with women's organisations, specifically Rape Crisis and Women's Aid, as well as addressing the ways that researchers have generated impact in educational settings. In discussing this, the chapter focuses on Lombard's work with school teachers in Scotland, as well as on work within universities, such as the Bystander Intervention project at the University of West England. In the area of gender, violence and abuse research, collaborations with police – both at the force level and with the Association of Chief Police Officers (ACPO) – have been used to change and improve policies. This will also be discussed within this chapter, as will the successful collaborations between researchers and people working in the field, such as practitioners and activists. Here the chapter focuses upon recent work in which such collaborations have facilitated policy change in a) extreme pornography and 'rape porn,' and b) restorative justice approaches to rape.

Background

As Bannister and Hardill argue, 'The "impact agenda" actively encourages the social sciences to make and demonstrate a difference; to justify and protect social science funding' (Bannister and Hardill, 2013, p. 167). Within research there is increasing emphasis on evidence-based practice: the development of responses and initiatives based on empirical research evidence. This provides opportunities for academics to work collaboratively with practitioners and to guide the direction of policy and practice.

Boswell and Smith (2017) identify two major incentives for social researchers in the UK to demonstrate that their research influences policy (i.e., demonstrates impact):

1   Impact is used to assess the quality of completed research. The UK's national research assessment framework, known as the Research Excellence Framework (REF), is used to assess universities' research output, with 'impact' forming one part of this REF assessment. The higher the REF impact score, the higher the amount of funding that is allocated to a University.

2   Impact is used to assess applications for future research funding. The majority of national, and international, researcher funders require researchers to dedicate significant amounts of space in grant applications to detailing how their research will have impact, both within and outside the research community.

In addition to these incentives, the need for practice to be rooted in research evidence has created impetus, and opportunities, for researchers to directly feed into practice developments. Evidence-based practice (EBP) (also referred to as knowledge exchange, knowledge utilisation and knowledge production) has been given increasing priority over the last three decades and has been described by Pawson (2006) as this millennium's 'big idea.' The need to integrate research findings and evidence with policy and practice has been given different levels of priority across different disciplines. The fields of medicine and health sciences have arguably taken this concept onboard to the greatest extent, but it has also received prominence in social work and other social science disciplines and areas of practice. This focus on EBP is grounded in the 'what works' agenda, which has driven, and been driven by, the need to develop policy and practice which is evidence-based.

Broadly speaking, evidence-based practice or knowledge exchange requires both collaboration between researchers and 'users of knowledge' throughout the process, and clear integration of research findings with practice or policy outcomes (Kothari and Wathen, 2013). This has changed over time, from what was previously a one-way linear process to more nuanced, multi-dimensional approaches (MacGregor et al., 2014). As Kothari and Wathen note, such knowledge exchange 'is being aggressively positioned as an essential strategy to address the problem of underutilization of research-derived knowledge' (Kothari and Wathen, 2013, p. 187).

Conducting research which has implications for both policy and practice has been at the core of feminist research since the 1970s. One of the primary principles of feminist research has been about doing research *about women, with women* and *for women* (see Chapter 2). This has been reflected in the epistemology and methodology of feminist research, as well as in its strong links with activism and practice. The overriding aim has been to use knowledge to expose and address the inequality women face, and to promote the economic, social and political status of women (Abraham and Purkayastha, 2012).

Gender, violence and abuse researchers therefore can, and do, influence policy direction and developments in a number of ways. Whilst not an exhaustive list, the following sections showcase some of the ways researchers have used their findings to influence and improve policy and practice.

Developing new ways of framing and naming violence and abuse

Although concepts and theorising on violence and abuse is often considered of most benefit to academics, developing new ways of defining and understanding forms of violence against women is an important element of policy development. As Abraham and Purkayastha (2012) state,

> Feminist conceptualization and methodologies are then translated by researchers to the specific arenas in which they seek to affect change, including, but not limited to the contexts of families, work and the economy, health, education, migration, violence, law, and government policies.
>
> (Abraham and Purkayastha, 2012, p. 128)

Liz Kelly's continuum of violence is perhaps one of the most well-known concepts in gender, violence and abuse, and is a particularly good example of the integration between research and practice. Following Kelly's research in the 1980s which explored women's experiences of sexual violence, she introduced the concept of the continuum in 1988. The purpose of the continuum was to move beyond discrete categories of violence, which was common across legislation, research and policy/practice at the time, to instead recognising that women experience a range of violence on a daily basis. Rather than being episodic, these violences intersect and overlap and are defined by commonalities, namely coercion, abuse and assault which is used to control and limit women. Kelly's continuum of violence offered a new framework for observing and understanding violence against women, framing it not as something that was rare or episodic, but normative and functional, occurring in the everyday context of women and girls' lives. This new framework allowed research, policy and practice to incorporate and examine the full range of violence women experience by men and to make the links between these, providing a deeper understanding to inform both prevention and response. It has informed practice in social work (Wendt and Moulding, 2016), as well as in women's organisations. The notion of a continuum of violence has also been adopted by the United Nations (UN, www.ohchr.org/Documents/Issues/Women/WRGS/SexualHealth/INFO_VAW_WEB.pdf) and by the Scottish Government (www.gov.scot/resource/doc/925/0063070.pdf).

Another example of the translation between research and practice can be seen in the work of Evan Stark who developed the concept of 'coercive control' to describe the features that underpin violence against women, particularly when it takes the form of domestic violence/intimate partner violence. This concept has now been incorporated into definitions of violence, including the cross-government UK definition of domestic violence and abuse. In England and Wales, a specific crime of Coercive Control was added to the Serious Crime Act 2015, placing the definition and concept of coercive control on a statutory footing. More recently, the work of McGlynn and Rackley (see example below) has informed the development of new policies to tackle image-based sexual abuse (IBSA).

Example: developing a concept of image-based sexual abuse

The work of McGlynn and Rackley highlights the ways in which empirical and conceptual research can influence policy. Over the last decade these researchers have focused on developing new ways of understanding and responding to extreme pornography and revenge pornography. One of the key outputs of this work has been the development of a new concept – 'image-based sexual abuse' – which encompasses the distribution and creation of private sexual images without consent. This concept captures the extent and nature of non-consensual creation or distribution of private sexual images, describing the phenomenon better than related terms such as 'revenge porn,' which has limited descriptive power as it only covers abuse that has been committed for specific purposes. McGlynn and Rackley's research has described the problem, identified some of its harms and outlined options for legal redress (civil and criminal laws).

Their REF impact case study describes how this research has led to a range of policy impacts (available online at http://impact.ref.ac.uk/CaseStudies/CaseStudy.aspx?Id=11804). They have used their findings to provide evidence to a number of national reviews and committees, including the House of Lords and Scottish Parliament. The following list highlights some of the ways the concept of image-based sexual abuse and its underpinning research have been used to effect change:

- McGlynn and Rackley's evidence was used by the Scottish Parliament in a Justice Committee report on the introduction of new laws covering abusive behaviour (Scottish Parliament Justice Committee, 2016). Their research was used to illustrate why criminal law covering image-based sexual abuse was needed and why the term 'revenge porn' was inadequate.
- McGlynn's work has been quoted in an Irish Law Reform Commission report on why anonymity is necessary for victim-survivors (Law Reform Commission, 2016).
- The term 'image-based sexual abuse' has been taken up academically as well as being used in public debates. For example, Maria Miller MP used it in Parliament, The Telegraph and other media platforms have used it and, critically, victims-survivors now use it to describe their experience. The term has been used by Women's Aid and by the All Party Parliamentary Group on Domestic Abuse report into online abuse.

Influencing the ways that violence and abuse is (or isn't) measured

Linked to the importance of research influencing the way violence and abuse is defined and named, is how different forms of abuse are counted and measured. As discussed in Chapter 5, national victimisation surveys are one of the most common forms by which national data on the prevalence of violence against women is collected. In England and Wales, the Crime Survey for England and Wales (CSEW) has collected data on various forms of gender-based violence (mainly domestic violence, sexual violence and stalking) since the mid-1990s. Academic research has contributed to the development and refinement of this survey. Walby has conducted extensive research examining survey methodologies, including the CSEW. Based on a recent large-scale project funded by the ESRC, Walby and colleagues examined the utility and limitations of the survey (Walby et al., 2015). They highlighted a number of issues with the survey, including the 'victimisation cap' (5 incidents) which meant that repeat victims were not being captured by the survey. Their work fed into the Office for National Statistics Steering Committee of Review of Domestic Abuse Statistics which led in turn to changes in the survey. These changes allowed for the accommodation of respondents who experience a high number of incidents.

Similarly, the authors of this book have drawn attention to the fact that the CSEW has traditionally excluded people aged 60 and over from participating in the self-completion module on domestic violence, sexual victimisation and stalking. The authors' work on sexual violence against older people demonstrated the problems associated with the exclusion of this age group, and led to the development of an evidence base which drew on police recorded data to examine the prevalence of sexual violence against older people. Their work contributed to the Office for National Statistics' decision to carry out a trial in which the age-cap for the self-completion module was lifted. This age-cap has now been permanently lifted to 74 for the self-completion module (ONS, 2018).

Informing interventions and programmes

Gender, violence and abuse research findings are often used to inform the development of interventions and programmes which seek to reduce violence. In some cases, researchers work with agencies or organisations to specifically design interventions or programmes as part of the research project. In other cases, a programme is developed after completion of the research, either by external organisations or in combination with the researchers. An example of the latter concerns Hester's work on gender and domestic violence perpetrators (Hester et al., 2006; Hester, 2009). The findings from her research have been used by the national organisation Respect (the UK membership association for domestic violence perpetrator programmes and associated support services) to inform training materials and presentations which are then disseminated to a range of professionals and practitioners[1]

A further example of the use of research findings to inform practice is the Intervention Initiative at The University of West England (UWE). UWE conducted research in 2014–2015 funded by Public Health England (Fenton et al., 2016). The research consisted of an evidence review. Overall, the authors reported that bystander intervention approaches can be useful in addressing primary prevention of violence against women in university settings. They found that programmes with social norms components were more likely to be effective if they were comprehensive, sufficient in length and duration, underpinned by theory, socio-culturally relevant and evaluated for effectiveness. Importantly, they should also be administered by well-trained staff. The researchers found that the process of achieving change is complex and requires time; the ability of short, one-off interventions to effect behaviour change is limited. Based on this, the UWE introduced 'The Intervention Initiative' – a programme of eight facilitated sessions, each lasting for 60 minutes (minimum) to 90 minutes (Fenton et al., 2014). The content of each of the sessions is provided in the form of facilitator notes, PowerPoint slides and handouts. The resource is free to use and is aimed primarily at higher education institutions.

A further example of the use of research to inform training programmes is Nancy Lombard's work on attitudes of primary school children towards violence against women (see example 2 below).

Example: changing the attitudes of school children to men's violence against women

Lombard's research into the attitudes of school children to men's violence against women found worrying attitudes to violence and gender equality (Lombard, 2008, 2011, 2013, 2014). Young people defined 'real' violence as physical acts done by men which had legal consequences; as much of the violence experienced or perpetrated by themselves did not fit this narrow construction, they minimised and normalised this behaviour. Worryingly, teaching staff also played a role in this minimisation. Lombard found that young people subscribed to naturalised definitions of masculinity to explain, rather than question, why men were violent. They justified men's violence against women using gender stereotypes and rigid, narrow understandings of adult relationship framed by heterosexuality and marriage. Consequently, they often blamed women for the violence and viewed it as a consequence of a woman not fulfilling her role.

Through personal communication, Lombard documents how her research featured in a number of debates in the Scottish Parliament and led to a collaboration with the Glasgow City Council Education Department in which a programme of training on gender equality was delivered in five schools who agreed to pilot the sessions. Following positive evaluation, the training was rolled out into a further ten schools. Following the development and expansion of this programme, further funding was awarded to facilitate the delivery of training sessions to members of staff (head teachers, teachers, educational practitioners, support staff and administrative staff) across 19 schools. The training was based on the research findings, and consisted of interactive sessions involving group activities and opportunities to ask questions. The training focused on the importance of gender, gender and violence, stereotypes and sexism, the ways in which schools contribute to the maintenance of the gender order, reflections on practice and practical guidance on taking learning from the session back into the classroom and everyday life.

As a result of this research, a number of organisations have developed similar training and programmes for professionals, including NHS Health Scotland who have developed a pilot to promote gender equal nurseries. This includes training for staff about the importance and relevance of gender equality via day-long training sessions. These sessions address the prevalence of gender stereotypes and the harm that these stereotypes cause.

Guides and training

A further way that gender, violence and abuse researchers inform policy and practice is via research briefing notes, guides and training toolkits. There is increasing emphasis on the importance of open access, and the need to share research
findings with audiences beyond the academic community. Many academics now
publish their work in open access journal articles as one way of achieving this.
However, platforms and methods which are specifically aimed at policy makers or
practitioners also represent an important tool for academics, as they allow them
to both to communicate their research *and* ensure that their findings can be fed
into policy and practice. Some of these platforms are described below.

- Briefing notes are commonly used in gender, violence and abuse research
  and can be aimed at either policy makers, practitioners, the general population or a combination of these. Recent examples include a briefing note on
  image-based sexual abuse (for more information see earlier example; https://
  claremcglynn.files.wordpress.com/2015/10/imagebasedsexualabuse-
  mcglynnrackley-briefing.pdf) and a briefing note written for the British
  Medical Association (BMA) titled 'Tackling Violence Against Women – Meeting
  Unmet Needs.'

  (Westmarland and Bows, 2018)

- Guides aimed at practitioners are often developed by researchers. For
  example, the authors of this book developed guides for age-related practitioners and sexual violence organisations based on Bows' doctoral research
  on the topic of sexual violence against people aged 60 and over.

  (available online at www.dur.ac.uk/criva/media/briefings/)

- Researchers often contribute to national guidelines, either directly through
  their research findings or by being involved as experts on panels which
  develop guidelines. For example, the joint Department of Health and Home
  Office's Victims of Violence and Abuse Prevention Programme involved a
  large number of violence and abuse academics as programme advisors and
  chairs of their expert groups. Similarly, the programme was directed by Professor Itzin – herself being an academic expert in violence and abuse.
- Consultations – government bodies, parliament and sometimes local government and councils will produce consultations where they ask experts in
  the chosen area to submit evidence. Over the last decade there have been
  an increasing number of these consultations on areas of violence against
  women. Recent examples in the UK include the All-Party Parliamentary
  Group (APPG) on Sexual Violence (March 2018), and the Sexual Harassment

of Women and Girls in Public Places Inquiry by the Women and Equalities Committee (June 2018). Both of these consultations received oral and written submissions from researchers on the topics of sexual violence in public and private places (Dr Maddy Coy and Dr Fiona Vera-Gray), and pornography (Professor Clare McGlynn and Dr Hannah Bows), as well as submissions from a range of specialist support services and activists.

- Developing training – in some cases, gender, violence and abuse researchers will use their research findings to develop training for practitioners and stakeholders (see example earlier in this chapter on Lombard's work training teachers). In other cases, researchers work with external organisations to develop training materials. This latter approach was adopted by one of the authors of this book (Westmarland). Westmarland and her collaborators Kate Butterworth and Maggie O'Neill worked together with Open Clasp Theatre Company to develop a play (Rattle Snake). The play was used to inform frontline police officers in how to respond to coercive control, and drew on the researchers' work on police understanding of coercive control (Westmarland and Butterworth), and expertise in arts-based research (O'Neill).

Summary

The use of academic research to inform policy and practice is increasingly important as the focus of research moves towards 'impact.' Gender, violence and abuse researchers have a long history of using research to support policy and practice developments in the area of violence against women. This chapter has provided an overview of some of the ways researchers can use their work to inform policy and support new areas of practice, ultimately resulting in 'real world' change.

Note

1 See impact case study, available at http://impact.ref.ac.uk/CaseStudies/CaseStudy.aspx?Id=40304).

References

Abraham, M. and Purkayastha, B. (2012) Making a difference: Linking research and action in practice, pedagogy, and policy for social justice: Introduction, *Current Sociology*, 60(2), pp. 123-141.

Bannister, J. and Hardill, I. (2013) Knowledge mobilisation and the social sciences: Dancing with new partners in an age of austerity. *Contemporary Social Science*, 8(3), pp. 167-175.

Boswell, C. and Smith, K. (2017) Rethinking policy 'impact': Four models of research-policy relations, *Palgrave Communications, 3*(44), pp. 1–10.

Fenton, R. A., Mott, H. L., McCartan, K. and Rumney, P. (2014) *The Intervention Initiative*. Bristol: UWE and Public Health England.

Fenton, R. A., Mott, H. L., McCarton, K. and Rumney, P. (2016) *A Review of Evidence for Bystander Intervention to Prevent Sexual and Domestic Violence in Universities*. London: Public Health England.

Hester, M. (2009) *Who Does What to Whom? Gender and Domestic Violence Perpetrators*. Bristol: University of Bristol and Northern Rock Foundation.

Hester, M., Westmarland, N., Gangoli, G., Wilkinson, M., O'Kelly, C., Kent, A. and Diamond, A. (2006) *Domestic Violence Perpetrators: Identifying Needs to Inform Early Intervention*. Bristol: University of Bristol, Northern Rock Foundation and Home Office.

Kothari, A. and Wathen, C. N. (2013) A critical second look at integrated knowledge translation, *Health Policy, 109*(2), pp. 187–191.

Law Reform Commission (2016) *Harmful Communications and Digital Safety*. Dublin: Law Reform Commission.

Lombard, N. (2008) 'It's wrong for a boy to hit a girl because the girl might cry': Investigating primary school children's attitudes towards violence against women, In: F. Alexander and K. Throsby (Eds.) *Gender and Interpersonal Violence: Language, Action and Representation* (pp. 121–138). Basingstoke: Palgrave Macmillan.

Lombard, N. (2011) *Young People's Attitudes about Violence*. Centre for Research on Families and Relationships (CRFR) Briefing 54. Edinburgh: CRFR.

Lombard, N. (2013) Young people's temporal and spatial accounts of gendered violence, *Sociology, 47*(6), pp. 1136–1151.

Lombard, N. (2014) 'Because they're a couple she should do what he says': Young people's justifications of violence: Heterosexuality, gender and adulthood, *Journal of Gender Studies, 25*(3), pp. 241–253.

MacGregor, J. C., Wathen, N., Kothari, A., Hundal, P. K. and Naimi, A. (2014) Strategies to promote uptake and use of intimate partner violence and child maltreatment knowledge: An integrative review, *BMC Public Health, 14*(862), pp. 1–16.

Office for National Statistics (2018) *Methodology: Improving Crime Statistics for England and Wales – Progress Update July 2018. Latest Update on the Progress Being Made to Improve Crime Statistics for England and Wales*. Available from: https://www.ons.gov.uk/peoplepopulationandcommunity/crimeandjustice/methodologies/improvingcrimestatisticsforenglandandwalesprogressupdate

Pawson, R. (2006) *Evidence-Based Policy: A Realist Perspective*. London: Sage.

Scottish Parliament Justice Committee (2016) *Stage 1 Report on the Abusive Behaviour and Sexual Harm (Scotland) Bill*. SP Paper 885.1. Edinburgh: Scottish Parliamentary Corporate Body.

Walby, S., Towers, J. and Francis, B. (2015) *Technical Paper on the Methodology of the Crime Survey for England and Wales Relevant to an Analysis of the Changing Rate of Violent Crime*. Lancaster: Lancaster University.

Wendt, S. and Moulding, N. (Eds.) (2016) *Contemporary Feminisms in Social Work Practice*. Abingdon: Routledge.

Westmarland, N. and Bows, H. (2018) *Tackling Violence Against Women –Meeting Unmet Needs*. London: British Medical Association. Available from: https://www.bma.org.uk/collective-voice/policy-and-research/public-and-population-health/womens-health

12 Afterword

In this book we have documented some of the most common methods used to research gender, violence and abuse and the how these methods can be used to uncover new knowledge and advance existing understandings of gender, violence and abuse. Within these chapters we have showcased innovation in methods through case examples of researchers exploring different forms of violence and abuse across different contexts. In these closing words we offer a brief overview of the key contributions of this book and consider future directions in researching gender, violence and abuse.

We started this book by positing that few researchers would cite research methods as being the most exciting part of social research. However, the examples given in this book have shown that using the most appropriate methods, in the most exciting way possible, can produce new knowledge in areas of gender, violence and abuse – particularly in topics that are in need of empirical and theoretical development. This theoretical development has a knock-on effect, as shown in Chapters 10 and 11, to policy, practice and activism. We have showcased a range of exciting approaches to research and have intentionally drawn on many examples from early career researchers and PhD researchers who are at often at the forefront of methodological and theoretical developments.

Our academic sisters in the 1970s–1990s focused on making visible the problems with traditional, mainly quantitative methods to investigate predominantly male-related social problems. They sought to show another way of doing research – debates that go to the heart of feminist epistemological and ontological concerns. Today's feminist scholars are building on this early work and developing new ways of researching gender, violence and abuse – new ways of knowing. Whilst qualitative interviews and focus groups (Chapter 5) continue to be some of the most common methods in research, there are now a suite of other qualitative, and quantitative methods, at a researcher's disposal including ethnography (Chapter 9), arts-based and other creative methods (Chapter

7). Increasingly, researchers are utilising existing data, generated either by previous academic research or from other sources such as the media, to answer new research questions (Chapter 8).

Moreover, technology is enabling more traditional methods (such as interviews and surveys) to be conducted in new ways. This is important, as it extends the scope of research and potential samples much further; those who have traditionally been under-represented in research, for example because of geographical location, language, disability or health, may now be able to participate in research that utilises the internet to communicate and collect data. In some cases, it reduces the financial costs of doing research, as well as the environmental costs of travel and the personal/family costs of spending long periods of time away from home.

We discussed in Chapter 7 how arts and creative methods are being used to research violence and abuse against those who have been less visible in previous research. These methods take a wide range, including dance, poetry, music, drama, photography, drawing, painting, sculpture and other creative methods such as quilting. In this chapter we show how these methods are growing in popularity and are enabling researchers to communicate with those who may not be able, or want to, take part in research using other methods such as surveys or interviews. These methods are particularly useful when working with children, or with people who do not speak the same language as the researcher. Diversity in research – in participants but also in terms of the researchers – is increasingly important and has the ability to take knowledge in new and often unanticipated directions.

However, these methods do not need to be used in isolation and increasingly researchers are combining methods (mixed methods) to quantify violence and abuse (through quantitative methods) as well as understand the nuances through qualitative approaches.

We discussed in Chapter 2 principles of feminist research which unify the various strands of feminist theory and methodology as set out by Beckman (2014). Among the principles are reducing power hierarchy, hearing the voices of survivors and conducting multidisciplinary research. We dedicated two chapters of this book to showcasing how researchers are working across disciplines to examine different forms of the violence and abuse, and the opportunities and challenges this presents (Chapter 4) as well as the relationship between activism and research (Chapter 10). Another core principle of feminist research is using research findings to create meaningful changes. In Chapter 11 we showed how researchers are using their research to inform policy and practice developments and create real world 'impact' to prevent violence and abuse and improve services for survivors.

A core principle of feminist research - though one which is not always realised - is ensuring research is intersectional. The concept of intersectionality, as developed by Crenshaw (1989, 1991), has been argued to be the biggest theoretical breakthrough in feminist research (McCall, 2005). However, this breakthrough has not yet been fully reflected in how it is incorporated into design and methods - we still have some way to go in this regard. Within the chapters of this book we have tried to showcase some of the exciting research being conducted which is intersectional in design and focus, however there is more to be done to ensure that all violence and abuse research is grounded in the principles of intersectionality.

Violence and abuse continues to be a major global issue, affecting millions of women and girls, and to a lesser but nonetheless still significant number of men and boys. These principles, combined with continued innovation through the new generation of researchers makes researching gender, violence and abuse an exciting scholarly topic and gives us hope for the future in terms of this translating into a future free from violence and abuse.

References

Beckman, L. J. (2014) Training in feminist research methodology: Doing research on the margins, *Women & Therapy, 37*(1-2), pp. 164-177.

Crenshaw, K. (1989) Demarginalizing the intersection of race and sex: A black feminist critique of antidiscrimination doctrine, feminist theory, and antiracist politics, *University of Chicago Legal Forum, 140*(1), pp. 139-168.

Crenshaw, K. (1991) Mapping the margins: Intersectionality, identity politics, and violence against women of color, *Stanford Law Review, 43*(6), pp. 1241-1299.

McCall, L. (2005) The complexity of intersectionality, *Signs: Journal of Women in Culture and Society, 30*(3), pp. 1771-1800.

INDEX

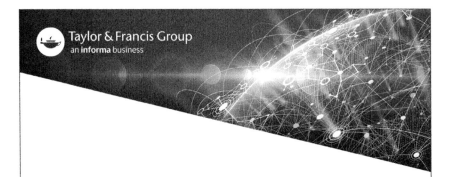